IVORY TOWERS IN THE MARKET PLACE

Ivory Towers in the Market Place

THE EVENING COLLEGE IN AMERICAN EDUCATION

By

JOHN P. DYER

Professor of History and Dean of University College
Tulane University

The Bobbs-Merrill Company, Inc.

Publishers

INDIANAPOLIS • NEW YORK

FIRST EDITION

To My Colleagues

in the AUEC

... it becomes expedient for promoting the publick happiness that those persons whom nature has endowed with genius and virtue, should be rendered by liberal education worthy to receive and able to guard the sacred deposit of the rights and liberties of their fellow citizens, and that they should be called to that charge without regard to wealth, birth or other accidental condition or circumstance ..."

—THOMAS JEFFERSON

Preface

PERHAPS a few words ought to be said about what this book proposes to be. The easiest way to say this seems to be first to indicate what it is not.

It is not a book about adult education in the broad and generic sense. Many books have already been written on this subject. Rather it is concerned with one important phase of American adult education—the university evening college. Above all, it is not a handbook for deans and directors on how to run an evening college.

This should be considered merely as a report on the evening college, its nature, its practices, and its problems, and a suggestion of what its role probably should be in our contemporary society. I very much hope it will be of interest to college and university presidents, boards of trustees, day deans, and faculties; to my colleagues in the field of university adult education; and to many interested lay people who ought to know something about what may well be the most important development in recent American higher education. If it can give these people a good overview of the evening college and can stir up some intelligent controversy and investigation, it will have served its purpose.

Because this is the first full-length book on the subject, I have been sorely beset with difficulties in writing it. Not only have I been deprived of the opportunity for the hidden plagiarism so often encountered in second and third books on a subject, but the problem of how to organize and present the material has plagued me. There is more than one way in which this might have been done; but I have chosen to describe separate facets of the evening college in the hope that in viewing the parts, the reader may see something of the whole. The evening college is an unknown world to many, even to educators. If there appears to be oversimplification at times, it is because I am anxious for lay people unaccustomed to pedantic jargon to see something of this new and rapidly developing phase of higher education.

A number of people have assisted in the preparation of this book. To them goes my appreciation. The staff of the Center for the Study of Liberal Education for Adults, Morton Gordon in particular, has materially assisted in the collection of data and has offered many suggestions for improving the manuscript. The manuscript itself has been read in part or in whole by Cyril O. Houle of the University of Chicago, Herbert Hunsaker of Purdue University, Robert A. Love of the City College of New York, Robert A. Blakely of the Fund for Adult Education, Frances Horn, President of Pratt Institute, Lawrence K. Frank of New York City, Leonard Reissman and T. T. Earle of Tulane University, Willis H. Reals of Washington University, and Frank Neuffer of the University of Cincinnati. They are not responsible for the final content and form of the book, however. This responsibility rests with me.

John P. Dyer

New Orleans, Louisiana
July 1955

CONTENTS

CHAPTER | PAGE

1 THE EVENING COLLEGE STUDENT 3

2 THE DEVELOPMENT OF THE EVENING COLLEGE 27

3 THE EVENING COLLEGE AND THE COMMUNITY 53

4 THE CURRICULUM—REAL AND IMAGINARY . . 81

5 DEAN AND FACULTY 112

6 A ROLE FOR THE EVENING COLLEGE 138

7 LIBERAL EDUCATION 168

NOTES 187

BIBLIOGRAPHY 196

INDEX 202

IVORY TOWERS IN THE MARKET PLACE

1 The Evening College Student

Take your movie camera with you on a visit to the campus of any one of a hundred-odd American colleges or universities any evening between six and ten, Monday through Friday. Photograph what you see. The chances are that when you and your friends see the film you will want to discuss the implications of what the visual record reveals, for here on the campus are new and exciting activities.[1] Where once the picturesque old night watchman trod his solitary rounds looking for those students who might be tempted to lurk in the shadows with those of the opposite sex, there are now a thousand men and women hustling from one class to another with much more than romance on their minds. Not that sex doesn't bob up now and then but hardly in such proportions as to give the dean of women cause for concern. The occasional young man with a faraway look in his eyes is probably simply wondering where the money is coming from for Junior's tonsillectomy. Once the library was a lighthouse in a shadow world of dark buildings and of trees making

3

giant patches against the starlit sky. Now the whole campus is ablaze with light. Every building clear to the top floor shows signs of people and activity.

In the campus coffee shop most uncollegiate-looking groups talk animatedly over coffee or sodas—talk and then break up as the bell for classes sounds—and their places are taken by other groups fresh from classes. It does not take a very discerning person to realize that the people in these groups don't conform to the stereotype of the average college or university student. True, one sees a few bobby soxers with their dirty saddle oxfords and a scattering of young men sloppily dressed as all true college men should be. But there is something distinctly different here. There is a middle-aged woman correct in her attire and prim in her pince-nez. One eye is on her hamburger and the other on a French grammar. Just a table away sit three young men of about thirty. There's no mistaking them. They have it written all over them that they are, or are in the process of becoming, junior executives, and they are taking themselves, their jobs, and the world frightfully seriously. Next to them, talking to a professional-looking man with guardsman mustachios (teacher or student? One can't tell the difference here), is a bronzed giant in T shirt and crew cut. A varsity tackle, one would guess, but the truth is he works for a construction company during the day and toward an engineering degree at night.

Take the camera into the classrooms and laboratories where students are working.

In the biology laboratory one sees the same heterogeneous group as he saw in the coffee shop. Peering intently into a microscope, almost oblivious to his surroundings, is a close-cropped, dark little middle-aged man. He is, one learns, pastor of an important church in the city. All his life, he told the dean at registration, he had wanted to know something of the world of science, but his life and education had been filled with theology, social studies, literature, and languages. Now he has the opportunity to indulge his craving for science—not for credit or a degree but for the sake of expanding his knowledge of the universe which is God's Kingdom. Near him, working with a bacterial culture, is a plumpish blond schoolteacher taking this course to fulfill degree requirements. And so one goes around the laboratory watching these adults work—a minister, a teacher, a would-be science-fiction writer, two medical technology students, a premedical student, a nurse, and three who are not quite sure why they are there.

In the personnel management class one instantly is attracted to Joe on the front row. He is thirty, dark and almost dapper with his thinly penciled mustache, and very intent. Joe, one learns, is the son of an immigrant Italian barber. When he finished high school he went to work in industry instead of going to college, but he soon found his lack of education was a barrier between him and where he wanted to go; so he chose the evening college as a way to get somewhere in a hurry. He goes to classes five nights a week while his wife sits home with the baby. His grades? He hasn't made below a "B" in any course; and his company has plans for him. "Joe is a smart one," his fellow workers say. "He'll go places." And Joe agrees with them, for he is not a particularly modest fellow.

Around Joe sit twenty other hopefuls of about the same age but maybe not so smart as he. All of them are seeking the magic formula which will make them managers of men; in adjoining rooms up and down the hall, scores of other young to middle-aged men and women are studying to be salesmen or accountants or junior executives or statisticians, or for any other of a hundred fields open to them. These are not underprivileged people. They are the people you see every morning and evening riding the busses and streetcars to and from work or car-pooling for the ride in from and back to Suburbia. They simply are urban dwellers and workers with ambition enough to seek a way of climbing a rung or two on the ladder leading up to a better life. Most of them dress very well and own cars, and many of them have made down payments on modest homes in the suburbs, which they will own in twenty years. Meantime, they can mow their lawns, water the flowers, and chat with neighbors across the fence while their wives cook dinners in well-equipped kitchens. These are the people who in returning to school "reflect a fundamental spirit of optimism," an optimism which drives them to achieve something which will save them from being "lost in a great anonymous faceless mass of humanity."[2]

Across the campus in the music building the professor is lecturing on symphonic music. On the blackboard is a drawing of the arrangement of a symphony orchestra—the strings, woodwinds, brasses, and percussion sections. Then recordings which bring out the significance of each section are played; first a movement, and then an entire symphony, the professor conducting and striking the blackboard sketch sharply at intervals with his baton to indicate the sections as they come into prominence. Sitting in the midst of a bevy of middle-aged women is a well-tailored, graying man viewing the entire procedure with some detachment. When asked why he is taking this course in music appreciation his reply is: "Well, my wife is a member of the Symphony Guild. She insists that I attend all the concerts with her, so I decided I might as well find out something about what a symphony is."[3]

Thus, behind the ivy curtain of traditional college and university education there is developing a new phase of higher education, vast in its implications and important in the services it renders. It is the university evening college, a hustling, vigorous institution, not yet mature, but conscious of its potentialities and characterized by an almost religious sense of its destiny. Every year approximately a quarter of a million adults enroll in the hundred-odd member institutions of the Association of University Evening Colleges. When there is added to this those enrolled in junior colleges and in institutions not affiliated with the association (extension centers, for example), the total probably would be more than a million.[4] It is a small wonder that the visitor to the campus at night is impressed by what he sees. Almost always he wants to discuss the implications of what he has seen and to ask questions, questions such as: Who are these people? Why do they come here night after night? How do they get along in their studies? How do they compare with day students? What are their peculiar problems, if any?

The evening college dean wishes he had the complete answers to all these questions, but he knows he hasn't. Only now are certain phases of these questions under investigation and some must wait for future studies. However, much is known and can be related.

Perhaps the first characteristic of the evening college is heterogeneity. One finds here many students who already have college degrees and others who have only finished high school. The age range is from eighteen to sixty-five or seventy, with the median age being thirty plus. One third is under twenty-five; 10 percent over forty-five. Some have excellent scholastic backgrounds and are constantly reading and learning, both in and out of college courses. Others are dull, fatigued, or lethargic, but somehow they have a will to learn and thus hang on, at times even after the dean has advised them to drop out. Some are taking courses for credit toward a degree and many are not, although the former are more prevalent. Social backgrounds vary, although most of them come from what the sociologist would call the middle and lower-middle class.

More important than this factor of hetereogeneity, however, is the matter of motivation. What impels these people to attend classes week after week, month after month, often at the expense of giving up a large part of their family and social-recreational life? Why are they willing to work for six to fifteen years for a degree? The evening college dean again wishes he had a complete answer. He knows there exist powerful motivating forces—that is self-evident—but what are they? Undoubtedly the need for vocational or semi-professional training stands high on the list. A man or woman wants to prepare for a better job or for advancement in the job now held. But it is becoming increasingly evident that there is another strong reason which the student finds difficult to explain clearly but which he obviously feels rather deeply. His nearest approach to any sort of rational verbalization goes something like this: "I just feel that I need a better education. I don't mean just to help me make more money. I mean—well, I just think more education would be good for me." Every evening college dean has heard this over and over again, and yet little is actually known about what such a student really means. Perhaps even the student himself doesn't know precisely what he is trying to say except that there is something in him which cries out for a better life, a life lifted out of the drab and routine. Perhaps he has learned that man does not live by bread alone. At any event this student constitutes perhaps the greatest challenge to the evening college, which must try to understand him and to provide the substance which will help give him a better life along with a better living, a liberal education if one chooses to call it that.

There are other motivations, of course. Some enroll because evening college is a good place to meet people and find companionship; others make a pleasurable hobby of evening college work; still others wish to overcome certain obvious personal culture deficiencies; some don't have a reason that anyone is able to discover. One might summarize the entire question of motivation by outlining the principal factors under the two large heads of: (*a*) life space areas and (*b*) life chance areas.[5]

Life space areas include the subjective element, the non-academic motivation in the area of social and psychological gratification. In the popular sense this might be called cultural (although the word is indefinite) motivation, for the important values are in the social and psychological areas and not in the economic. Perhaps it is man's search for intangible satisfactions in the boundless spatial dimensions of human wants and urges. Breaking this down into more precise and meaningful terms, one encounters numerous ingredients. There is, for example, *social conformity,* the desire of a person to do what his peer groups are doing. His peer groups have an education, or at least have been to college, so he goes to college. Thus, he hopes to find acceptance. Another factor is *social class mobility,* the desire to acquire social "know-how," information and orientations which will assist him to move to a higher social level or to move with greater assurance in his own circle. *Skill for role fulfillment* is another: the need to acquire skills in the performance of a recently acquired social role in which inadequacy is felt. With the birth of the first child, for example, a couple acquires a new role. The community leader who finds he is frequently called upon to speak in public may find it desirable to take courses in public speaking in order that he may be more effective in his role as leader. The *desire for new experiences* is also a factor. A man or woman may be bored, restless, lonely. He feels the need to fill gaps in his life, the exact nature of which he may not be able to identify but which he hopes to discover in the evening college. Finally, the *irrational and compulsive element* must be considered, for it is true that in some instances the emotionally disturbed may go to the evening college to get support for their ideas, to act out their neuroses or to rationalize their problems.

The life chance area is made up of the rational economic element—getting a better job, making more money, increasing one's chances, extending the field of choice of occupations. As in the case of life space areas, this area may also be broken down into subdivisions. *Vertical job mobility,* or the moving ahead on the job one has, is one part. The salesman expects to move into an executive position, for example, or the industrial worker wishes to move up to foreman. Each feels his need for more education if he is to succeed. *Horizontal job mobility* or the preparation for another job in a different line of work is another. The plumber takes courses in accounting because he wishes to enter that field, or the drug clerk wishes to study engineering. Still another is *delayed and undirected mobility,* in which a person wants a degree for no specific and immediate purpose, but because he feels that with a degree he can get ahead in his own immediate field or in some other field which he may select. This type of student is becoming more and more prevalent in virtually all the evening colleges. He is looking for some sort of investment for the future, some insurance that he may be ready when his big opportunity comes. Finally, there is *skill for economic role fulfillment*. The newly appointed foreman takes courses in leadership and personnel management because he realizes that in his new work he must learn or fail; or the bookkeeper promoted to auditor takes courses in analysis of financial statements for the same reason.

In the process of achieving these goals, as has been previously suggested, marked differences between the day and evening college student emerge. The average evening college student has been out of high school for a period of five to thirty years. Older than the day student, he is often much more highly motivated and more in earnest about what he is trying to do. His maturity plus the fact that most of his interests are focused somewhere other than on the campus makes him ordinarily only slightly interested in campus social and extracurricular life. He has problems which most of the day students have never experienced—earning a living, raising a family, for example. In the classroom he is likely to demand good teaching and is unwilling to put up with the dull lectures sometimes foisted upon the hapless day student. On the whole, the adult student is less impressionable than the young day student, but there is a broader background of experience upon which he draws. Absenteeism is somewhat more prevalent in the evening because of the demands made upon the student's time by his family, his job, or social obligations. For the same reasons he is likely to interrupt his work by dropping out for a term or so and then re-enrolling.

Certain differences are important in comparing the scholastic achievement of the two types of students. There are factors which place the evening student at a disadvantage. He does not have the time for as much study and library reading as the undergraduate day student is expected to put in. Because of the fact that he has been out of high school for several years he is likely to be "rusty" in certain fields, science and mathematics in particular. Fatigue also plays an important part in any lack of success he may have, for ordinarily he comes to classes in the evening after a full day's work. His remoteness from campus life also makes it difficult for him to associate with his fellow students and to have proper conferences with his instructors.

The extent to which these factors exist and the degree to which they are compensated for by higher motivation, greater maturity and experience, and more intensive effort are conjectural. Inadequate evidence indicates that the negative factors may not be as important as a reading of the list tends to show. Not all of them can be eliminated, but some may. Stimulating teaching on an adult level helps overcome the fatigue factor; a slight change in the method of checking out library books can obviate the necessity of the student's spending long hours in the library (placing books on overnight reserve, for example, almost completely restricts their use by evening students); and it is doubtful if the evening college student is much "rustier" in basic subjects than many entering freshmen in the day colleges.

The question of whether adults *can* learn or not seems well settled. *They can.* The true situation has perhaps been somewhat obscured by "a polar argument between those who believe that childhood is the optimal period of learning and those who just as adamantly hold that adults are superior learners."[6] One bases its arguments on the results of tests which indicate that peak learning takes place roughly between twenty and twenty-six years of age. The argument from another side comes largely from anecdotal material about the age at which great creative minds have best functioned. Between these views lies what appears to be the truth about adult learning.

Freeman has written that the evidence shows that "although there is a very slight decline between the ages of approximately thirty and fifty, the loss is not very serious; and, it may be urged, the loss is perhaps more than compensated for by accrued experience, better organization of intellectual behavior, and improved judgment." To this he adds: "After the age of sixty, a somewhat more marked rate of decline seems to take place."[7] Pressey, Janney, and Kuhlen have added their corroboration to Freeman's findings.[8] At Iowa State College, studies indicate mental ability is probably greater at fifty than it is at thirty.[9]

From the foregoing it would appear that there are factors more important than age in the learning process. Kuhlen was frank to admit this was true in a faculty seminar at Syracuse University in May of 1954.[10] According to him:

1. The factor of disuse may well be more important than age.

2. The curve shows only the *peak* of learning ability. But this is not so important because people seldom have to call upon the maximum of their learning powers. We can usually get along on something less than the peak power. For example, adults obviously *run* less effectively than they did

ten years ago, but they *walk* just about as effectively as they did then.

3. Age is only one factor in learning ability. Other factors appear to be much more important—e.g., interest, motivation, and a host of intangibles that make for effective production and learning. Hence, data suggest that a person's peak age for efficiency of work production does not correspond with his peak age for learning (twenty to twenty-six years) but occurs between ages thirty to forty years.

Furthermore, cultural factors appear greatly to affect the ability-to-learn curve. For example, the learning-ability tests given to servicemen clearly show that between World War I and World War II there was throughout the adult population an increase in the ability to learn. It is reasonable to suppose that this increase may have resulted from enhanced verbal skills caused by the increased influence of mass media as well as from advance of common schooling. Studies also show the sharp impact of other cultural factors.

There are some differences, of course, due primarily to age.[11] For example, age directly affects physical efficiency, a man reaching the peak of his physical powers about the age of thirty. Age also affects sensory acuity. As one grows older, there is a loss of resiliency. There are greater needs of physical comforts, facilities for rest, need for better lighting than that needed earlier. And, of most importance, age changes are correlated with changes in personality and motivation.

Kuhlen identified the following phenomena as being of major importance in adulthood:

1. *Inertia.* Adults do not easily change their habits or attitudes. But Kuhlen remarked: "Despite this, it does seem that there is a growth-urge that persists throughout life."

2. *Goal change.* Adult goals do change; needs change; and roles change. Vocational advance seems to give way to cultural concerns. As an adult grows older, he seems to need "something more" than vocational satisfactions.[12] The kind of work done seems to be quite influential in determining the *kind* of changes that take place.

3. *More realism.* Adults want educational experiences that are realistically related to daily problems. They are more realistic than undergraduates. Short courses seem more desirable than semester-long courses. And there is evidence to suggest that adults seek educational experiences other than lectures, formal courses, and the like.

4. *Conflicting pressure.* As compared with adolescents, adults are subjected to many more conflicting pressures. For example, an adult may experience a pressure to go to school for job advancement, but at the same time experience a great pressure to be at home at night to help care for the children or a sick wife. Kuhlen suspects that the serious drop-out rate in adult education is due more to these conflicting pressures than to the quality of the educational experience.[13]

5. *Changes in time perspective.* There does come a time or a point at which adults view their future as *now*. Attempts to extend the future occur by means of such things as interest in genealogy, identification with their children, or with increased concern with immortality. Advancing age brings about a decrease in many kinds of activities, but church activity holds up and often increases. This, according to Kuhlen, makes the church a very important agency of adult education.

6. *Tendency to be threatened.* As age advances, adults appear to be easily threatened by change and by tests of one's

capacity. These tendencies to be threatened often lead to the avoidance of behavioral change. Unknown ventures are initially unwelcomed; situations loaded with the unexpected are avoided. Kuhlen feels that these threatening tendencies call for: (*a*) Experiences and programs which will help this adult to be forward-looking, and (*b*) Teachers of adults who will be sensitized to these existing tendencies of adults to be or to feel threatened.

From material such as the above and from his own study, Siegle has concluded that there ought to be constructed a new graphic representation to replace the traditional learning curve.[15] He would represent it thus:

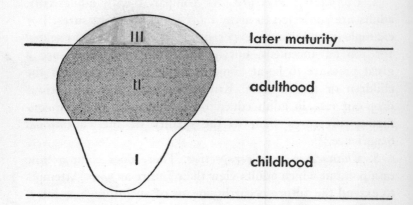

This schematic design has the virtue of clearly reflecting the bimodal nature of adult learning. The vertical thrust is the *level* of learning and the horizontal thrust is the *kind* of learning. By the level of learning, of course, it is meant the level of complexity of the tasks, particularly symbolic, which the individual can perform. Kinds of learning would include all kinds of motor, verbal, and social skills; a variety of subject matter areas; systems of thought; values and attitudes; sensory and perceptive habits—in short, all of those factors which are modifiable through learning experiences at any stage of life. With this in mind the reader may note the upward and outward expansion and contraction of learning ability from early childhood to old age.

The question which naturally follows is: *Do* adults learn? That is, do adults in college learn complex symbolic tasks as well as younger students in the day colleges?

The question is inevitable in the light of the increasing importance of the evening college in American higher education, and it ought to be answered. We are confronted with a state of affairs where many skeptical day college faculty members charge the evening college with soft pedagogy and low standards of scholastic achievement. At the same time the evening college dean and faculty are likely to make extravagant claims about the superior achievement of the evening college student. As a matter of fact, neither is on very solid ground, for the problem has not been seriously explored. This does not mean, however, that we are completely in the dark, for there are fairly reliable data based on objective observation and limited investigation. The following tentative random conclusions based on reports of faculty members who teach both day and evening students, and on the results of tests run by individual institutions, seem to summarize about what we know:

The superior adult student is as good as or better than the superior day student; the average students in both classifications are about equal; the poor student in the evening college is likely to be considerably poorer than his contemporary in the day college. Evening college students on the whole find difficulty with science, mathematics, and languages, and are likely to excel in history, political science, the social studies, and the humanities. Graduates of the evening college who go on to take postgraduate degrees seem to do as well as the day college graduates (undoubtedly because only the superior student in both categories is ordinarily admitted to graduate school). The evening college student is more likely to ask intelligent questions and to want to get at the root of things. When evening college students cross-register and take courses in the day colleges, no significant handicaps appear. Conversely, the day college student who takes work at night ordinarily makes about the same sort of record as in the day college.

In short, it may well develop upon exhaustive investigation that there is no significant difference in all-round scholastic achievement between the two categories of students. It also appears that part of the prejudice against the evening student may arise out of certain teaching situations: (a) The day faculty member teaches only occasionally in the evening college and on these occasions is unfortunate enough to get a class composed largely of poor students. (b) The day teacher is unsympathetic toward adult education and is unable or unwilling to adjust his teaching to the adult level. As a result he gets little response from his class and is likely to classify all evening students as inferior.

An interesting study along these lines has recently (1954) been made at Roosevelt University by the staff of the Center for the Study of Liberal Education for Adults.

Twenty-four pairs of day and evening college students were selected from the registration records of the college. The students were matched on the basis of sex, equivalent credit hours completed (sixty hours), and ACE Psychological Test total scores. (The ACE test is given to every student who enters the degree program at the college.)

Academic *ability* as measured by the ACE examination was held constant. Academic *achievement* was measured by the Educational Service Sophomore Comprehensive General Culture Test. This examination, as most educators know, tests knowledge and understanding in several academic areas, e.g., history and the social studies, literature, fine arts, science, and mathematics.

The results of this portion of the study indicate that the soft pedagogy charge is not substantiated at Roosevelt University. The average percentile rank based on national norms on this examination for both day and evening college students was 70.

The study was extended further into the classroom. Instructors' records in four courses were made available. In each case, objective-type examinations were given to both day and evening college students completing the courses. The results indicate no significant difference in achievement between day and evening students. Indeed, evening college students seem to have done a little better than day students.

The study is, of course, too limited to use as a basis for resounding conclusions, but it is significant; it also is indicative of the type of study which ought to be made over and over again in other institutions until results are irrefutable one way or another.

Such matters as motivation, how adults learn, and how much they achieve are matters of the gravest importance. Psychological research, statistics, and charts help make these things clear. But none of these reflects the real "feel" and spirit of the evening college and its students. This can come only from knowing the students themselves, from being intimately associated with their failures, their triumphs, and their problems. From the files of evening college deans and directors come true life accounts; if some of these seem to be out of Horatio Alger, the reader will have to make the best of it, for there is no place in American life today where the virtues of ambition, courage, and intelligent hard work are yielding greater returns in the lives of many men and women than in the country's evening colleges. The sophisticate who insists that the American ideal as expressed by Alger is dead just doesn't know what he is talking about.

In an Eastern university the president, who was once the director of the evening division, was waiting one evening for the elevator. Near him was another man waiting for the same elevator. As men will do under such circumstances, they covertly looked each other over.

"You are a student in the evening college?" asked the president.

"Yep," said the student.

"How long have you been going to evening school?" queried the president.

"About seven years," answered the student. "How long have you been here?"

"Well—let's see," mused the president, "about seventeen years, I guess."

"Oh, I see," rejoined the student. "You are working for a degree."

Among the G.I.'s who enrolled at the urban college of a Southern university was a huge, bearded, heavyweight wrestler whose name is known to sports fans all over the nation. He liked things around the college all right, but he just couldn't understand all the fuss over little things, commas, for example. Why should educated men like his instructors fool away so much time with little things? He just never got onto that, so commas became his bête noire. Now psychology—that was different. After about three weeks in class he heaved his three hundred pounds to a standing position and to his instructor, the class, and the world at large declared himself as follows: "Why, Doc, I been using this thing all my life. I just didn't know what to call it!"

In a Southwestern city, Charline finished high school and then took a business course fitting her for a secretarial position. For eight years she worked as a secretary in a large department store. She had dreamed of going to college, but somehow there never was enough left of her pay check for her to put by the necessary savings which would make it possible for her to resign and enroll full time in the college of her choice. Finally in 1950, she determined to work for her degree the hard way—at night. But she was not content to take just a light load. Every semester, including the summer, she took from nine to twelve hours and still did her forty-hour-a-week regular job. This schedule required four evenings per week in class and a lot of reading and studying on week ends. She also found that mornings from 5:30 to 8:00 made a very convenient study period.

Charline graduated *summa cum laude,* majoring in history. She fulfilled all requirements for a teaching certificate in her home state and then, to her joy and amazement, received a Fulbright Scholarship. In October 1954 she entered an English university for a year of graduate study.

Eileen finished high school at eighteen in a Midwestern city. She, too, decided to work and take her education in the evening college. She was fired with an insatiable, almost fanatical desire to be a medical doctor. The dean of the evening college tried to dissuade her, but to no avail. She was going to become a doctor if it killed her. She lived on the west side of the city and the college was on the east side, so she bought a car for commuting. By scrimping and saving she was able to keep up the payments with a little left over for tuition. But Eileen didn't last very long. During her first semester her grades were fair, but during the second semester she made a very poor showing, particularly in science. Came the next semester and she did what so many like her do. She simply didn't show up again and without a word to anyone slipped quietly into the oblivion from which she came.

Bob is an up-and-coming young buyer for a large department store in a Pacific Northwest city. He has a nice home, a good job, a fine family of six, and excellent prospects for the future. One thing he felt he lacked, however, and that was an education. Frequent buying trips to Europe as well as in the United States had not only convinced him that he needed an education but had shown him the sort of education he needed. He was doing well with his work and felt he needed a general education rather than more work in business administration. He enrolled in the evening college to pursue such a course leading to a bachelor of arts degree. Like others he finds the best time to study is early in the morning between six and the time he goes to work around nine. Often he schedules an 8:00 o'clock class in the morning and then fills in with evening work; and it is all adding up to a degree. But it isn't so much the degree, Bob says, as it is the fact that a man must know a great deal outside of his job to get along in the modern world. Moreover, his wife has fallen in with the idea, and the two of them have budgeted their time to allow for work, recreation, social activities, civic activities, and school.

Ray is an accountant with a firm in a Southern city. He would like to become certified, for it would mean additional income for him and the chance for a partnership in the firm. With this in mind he enrolled in the evening division of the university and set out on his program with high hopes. During his second semester he was irregular in attendance and his grades slipped to a bare passing mark. In the middle of his third semester he dropped out entirely, and when the dean investigated he found what is so often the problem of the evening college student—family difficulties and financial pressure. In Ray's case his wife Ruth was pregnant with her first child. It was a hysterical pregnancy, with Ruth imagining every calamity under the sun which might befall her. She whined and whimpered about being left alone so much at night. She demanded medical attention from a specialist, so that her husband had to work nights and Sundays to make enough to pay the doctor bills. When her baby came she was even more unreasonable about her husband's attending evening classes. Now she became a real martyr, so Ray gave up.

James is a top research engineer in a large Midwestern city. In 1937 he finished high school and went to work as draftsman in a large industrial plant. Since 1938, except for two years in the Navy, he has been hammering away at an engineering degree in the evening division of a Midwestern university. At the same time he has been carrying a full-time job in industrial research. His life has been a closely scheduled pattern of classes and job promotions, until in March 1953 he was made head of the engineering section in his plant, which is concerned with the development of automobile air conditioning. In June 1954 he received his bachelor of engineering degree after having worked for it for nearly fifteen years. During those years he has found time to participate in civic affairs, to teach a Sunday School class, and to patent twenty inventions in the field of refrigeration. How did he do it? He gives the credit to his wife Betty. She's the one, he says, who shouldered the responsibility of looking after the family of two boys while he worked and went to school.

The director of a Midwestern school of commerce sends a report which is so graphic it is presented here just as he wrote it:

It is easy enough to put down in black and white what the records say about this woman who came to our evening college. She went to high school in the South and graduated in 1909. Her first courses with us were in salesmanship and personnel administration, two evenings a week in the spring of 1946—a very prosaic beginning. Here was someone with a special, quite practical interest or need who might take another course in retail merchandising and perhaps public speaking and then go on her way.

But that is not what the record shows. From two evenings a week her program expanded to three; and threads of English, philosophy, history, psychology and sociology began to be woven around a pattern that spelled serious interest in personnel work. The record is impressive enough. It extends over a period of six and one-half years, setting down the verdict of teacher after teacher that this student is "good," which is a very pale term to use to describe what it means to acquire an average of B. It is a beautifully consistent record as records go, culminating in the statement that its compiler has qualified for the Bachelor of Business Administration degree.

The white card with all this on it has taken its place with thousands of others in the files. But how little it really tells. It cannot speak of the widow whose son was fighting in the Pacific while she dispensed merchandise over the counter by day and came to school in the evenings. Perhaps it is unfair to record keeping to point out its limitations; for did it not tell us her age and the fact that she has been married? But not even a picture could catch the warmth and sparkle of a personality that manifested such friendly interest in fellow-students and so often gave them wise, unofficial counsel on studies and job. Nor do school records plot the brilliant progress from sales clerk to training staff and eventual supervision of personnel. And who but those who were there at the table with this woman and her handsome son and daughter-in-law at the graduation banquet could possibly sense what evening education meant to grandma when she came to receive her diploma?

By all the measuring devices we have, Charles is just plain no good. Before World War II he was successively enrolled in the college of liberal arts and in the school of commerce. In both he barely managed to eke out grades which would save him from dismissal. He went to the army and came back eligible for college work under the G.I. bill, so he promptly enrolled in the evening division. During the day he sold automobiles, or at least he pretended to sell them. Now and then a customer would, in spite of him, buy a car, and thus he held on with his company in the same way he had in college. He takes work in the evening college, but no one can figure why except perhaps to get the small stipend for which he has qualified. He is affable, with a disarming grin, and is wholly impervious to counseling. His grades are poor but not poor enough to exclude him. He is the despair of the dean, who upon hearing the student's name just lifts his eyes plaintively to heaven and mutters, "What the hell does one do with a guy like that?"

Contrast him with Dave, another G.I. Dave had, as he expressed it, "played around" in college before he went to the army. Now he was back, a somewhat sobered young man who was beginning to realize that life was much more than beer and skittles. His record in the day college before the war was rather poor, and besides he had a wife now and a baby on the way. He couldn't go back to college full time even if he had had the inclination, which he didn't. Instead, he took a job with an investment firm and enrolled in the evening college for courses which he thought would help him. One course led to another, and eventually with what he could salvage from his old record he was well on the way to a degree. He took the degree and is destined for an official position in the company. He has continued to take a graduate course now and then and on the outside to read everything there is to read on investments. The consensus is that he probably knows more in his field than any one of his senior partners in his company. One semester out of each year he teaches a course in investment principles in his alma mater.

Having received the above answers, or partial answers as the case may be, to his original questions, the inquiring visitor is likely to want to know more. How long has this sort of thing been going on? Where and how did the evening college movement originate? How is the evening college organized and how does it function within the framework of the university?

These questions deserve the special answers given in the following chapter.

2 The Development
of the
Evening College

I T WAS perhaps unfortunate that this new and important phase of higher education should come to be characterized as a "movement," for if one accepts as a definition of a movement that it is a series of acts and events tending toward some one definite end, one had best have another look at this characterization. There is hardly one and only one definite end or purpose which even a majority of the university evening colleges as a group are trying to achieve, because all evening colleges are not engaged in the same undertakings. Perhaps this may be clarified by a rough functional classification of evening colleges[1] somewhat as follows:

1. *Technical.* There are a few evening colleges devoting their entire program to technical curricula, the most common ones being in architecture, electronics, and engineering in some form or other. Although some of these offer pro-

fessional degrees, many of them confine themselves to certificate programs of the technical institute nature but far above the trade school level.

2. *Commerce.* Evening colleges devoting themselves exclusively to offerings in the field of commerce and business administration are somewhat more numerous than the evening technical colleges. Most often they are outgrowths or appendages of the day college of business administration and have similar curricula. Most of them grant degrees in commercial subjects.

3. *Liberal Arts.* As in the case of commerce, the liberal arts evening college is a degree-granting offshoot of the day college, with similar or exact curricula and degrees. It often exists in a university on the same campus as the commerce evening college but with a separate identity and administrative organization.

4. *Noncredit.* This type of evening college offers a multiplicity of courses designed for the adult and offered without credit toward a degree. This closely resembles the type of work offered by the extramural departments of English universities except that in this country the work is by and large offered in residence on the university campus rather than by extension. Although there are few of this type of evening college, they have made significant contributions in adapting materials to the levels and interests of adults and in freeing them from the shackles of the academic tradition. Perhaps the best-known institutions in this category are the University of Chicago's University College and the Division of General Education at New York University.

5. *The Multidimensional.* Those in this classification are often (but not always) called "university colleges" because they cut across the day college lines and offer at least some

work in a number of fields, such as commerce, liberal arts, engineering, architecture, medical technology, nursing, etc. Usually degrees are offered in all except the fields of architecture and engineering. It is a form which is growing rapidly in favor with many universities because it makes possible the consolidation of all evening college work into one administrative unit, a situation which is likely not only to provide greater administrative efficiency but also to offer a better integrated program.

It would appear from this, then, that there are at least five different evening college movements. Within each of these there is further fragmentation. In the liberal arts classification, for example, there is a wide divergence of opinion over what liberal arts for adults ought to be. Practices range from a strict adherence to traditional courses prepared originally for adolescents to courses which are frightfully modern and mad. In engineering there are those who say in effect that what we need is more and more technical training. There are others who feel keenly the need for more liberal education in engineering, but who, as yet, are unable to do much about it. The noncredit people talk a great deal and rather proudly about learning for the sake of learning, without the customary diplomas and degrees, and then reward their students with certificates in lieu of diplomas. In commerce and business administration there are conflicts. There are colleges of commerce which are "orthodox" and limit their offerings to strictly vocational subjects with a slight bow toward liberalizing trends. In others the commerce program is hardly distinguishable from the liberal arts. In the multidimensional one finds all these problems and more.

If further evidence of diversity were needed, the matter of

nomenclature might be considered; and this is not a trivial matter, for the name may be an index to what the university really conceives the evening college to be. It may be a *college*, a *division*, just *classes*, a *program*, or a *session*.

For the one hundred members of the Association of University Evening Colleges there are thirty-three different names used. The most frequent one is "Evening Division." This is followed by "Evening College" and this by "University College." Some are named for men, such as McCoy College at Johns Hopkins and Millard Fillmore College at the University of Buffalo. Others are named for cities, such as Dallas College of Southern Methodist and Cleveland College at Western Reserve. On the whole, nomenclature is a potpourri, with such names as Intown College, Downtown College, College of Adult Education, School of General Studies, Diploma School, Evening College and Graduate Division, Community College, College of Special and Continuation Studies, Division of General Education, and Extension Division. One university apparently doesn't propose to venture far into the dark, for it has a Twilight School.

It appears at times that about all these fragmented segments of the evening college have in common is that they are all passionately interested in teaching something to adults of all ages, they have common administrative problems, and they are all members of a loose confederation called the Association of University Evening Colleges. This situation, of course, makes it easy for the critic to charge that evening college education is too amorphous to have any well-defined goals and purposes; but this charge is hardly fair or justifiable. It may well be that there is some, as yet undiscovered, central theme or role upon which all classifications can and should unite. Close scrutiny, however, reveals that the fragmentation in evening colleges is scarcely any greater than that which exists within the framework of day colleges. One would hardly speak of "the day college movement" because it is generally recognized that each segment has its own discrete functions and problems. Denominational and secular colleges often differ widely on the question of what a liberal arts curriculum should be. Moreover, the curricula of both may range from the classical prescribed to a mishmash of electives which may not add up to much of anything. Schools of commerce have reached no common ground on what their ideal curriculum should be and, on many problems, are about evenly divided. The same could be said for engineering, law, architecture, and the others. In fact, it is very doubtful if clarity of vision regarding goals and roles is the exclusive attribute of any segment of higher education in the United States.

As one looks at evening college education he becomes conscious of the fact that there have been certain rather well-defined periods in its growth. Perhaps a summary of these will help to clarify this important new phase of higher education in our contemporary society.

The first period would be from some date in the last quarter of the nineteenth century to 1939. This may well be classified as a period of origins, a period which is the despair of the historian who tries to fasten on something specific which he may use as a point of departure. There is no place on the map on which one may put his finger and say that this is where evening college education began, and no date on the calendar from which one may reckon the exact time. One must, therefore, begin with the generalization that evening college education as it exists today is the unforeseen culmination of a half century of effort on the part of many different types of educational organizations whose purposes were to carry education to the masses of people. Having said this, one may then quite properly examine some of these organizations and institutions.

The half century between 1875 and 1925 witnessed the appearance in American higher education of new and powerful urges and influences. The sheer multiplication of institutions of higher learning was little short of astounding. In this period of time some 604 full four-year colleges and universities were founded, nearly a third of the total number now in existence. Upon these as well as upon older institutions new influences beat down fiercely. The fact that intellectual life was becoming more professionalized and specialized was made apparent in the shift from the older apprenticeship system of training professional men to the professional school, and in the new facilities for graduate study in institutions with well-equipped libraries and laboratories, research seminars, and professors indoctrinated in the German ideal of systematic investigation within narrow areas. Expanding industry and commerce demanded the technical assistance of experts in administration, sales, science, and engineering; and they were willing to pay for it. University and college endowments increased enormously. The problems of the rapidly growing cities demanded trained sociologists, economists, and political scientists. Even the farm and farm life began to feel the effects of the research being conducted in the fields of bacteriology and soil chemistry.[2]

Along with this urge toward specialization and professionalization was another trend which had special relevance for the evening college, the attempts to popularize knowledge and take it to the man in the street. As Curti has pointed out, "the gulf between the knowledge of the intellectual and that of the common people has always been wide, everywhere, but it has been less wide in America than elsewhere."[3] It is in this fact that the unique characteristic of American intellectual and educational philosophy lies. In its simplest terms it may be called democratic education, as distinguished from the aristocratic concept one found in certain parts of Europe. It grew out of the belief that education was for everyone; that education was the best means of achieving success in a democratic society with a high degree of social mobility; that it could bridge all gaps.

This urge toward the popularization of knowledge may best be seen in the development of two types of academic institutions and one classification which, for lack of a better term, may be called nonacademic. The two academic developments were: (1) the municipal university and (2) the university extension service. The nonacademic is a montage of library associations, Chautauquas, YMCA's, lyceums and other lecture bureaus, popular books and magazines, reading circles, and even commercially motivated and operated correspondence and home study schools.

First to emerge, wilt, and then take on new growth was the university extension plan, which had its genesis in certain ideas being developed during the nineteenth century in England. First Cambridge during the 1870's and somewhat later Oxford put into practice an idea which had been germinating in many minds for how many years no one knew.[4] On its surface it was not a particularly recondite idea. It was simply: Why not take university education to people who cannot attend the university? But it was an idea likely to appeal to American universities fired with a zeal for more democracy in education. It was natural, therefore, that

American scholars should take steps to adapt the idea to American university education. Herbert Baxter Adams at Johns Hopkins and William Rainey Harper at Chicago were among the pioneering university presidents who developed early extension departments. Their lead was followed by many others. Soon there was a veritable flood of extension centers and classes all over the country, the content of the courses being as multipatterned as a landscape seen from an airplane. Any group in any part of the country could get just about anything it wanted, either intellectual or practical. State universities, land grant colleges, and privately endowed institutions vied with each other in prolificness of offerings. Truly it seemed that "a new era of Athenian culture was at hand."[5]

This period of flush times lasted until around the turn of the century when a decline set in which made it appear that extension education for adults was just a flash in the pan. The reasons for the decline cannot be related in detail here, but it seems significant for the evening colleges of today to mention two of the important ones. The early extension movement withered and almost died largely because it was not adequately financed and also because "the university professors failed to realize that mature adults might neither relish nor find profitable the diet prescribed for those in their late adolescence."[6] In other words, the universities themselves had not learned that any sort of permanent educational program must be put on a sound financial basis and that educational offerings must be placed on the level of the learner's interests and needs. As one reads of some of the astounding practices in the early extension movement one wonders how it survived at all. But it did survive and, following World War I, entered a period of renewed growth and vigor. During this period of recovery the evening college as an institution distinct from extension classes began to assume something of its present form.

Meantime, the municipal university idea was growing with the growth of the cities. Prior to 1875 only two municipal colleges or universities existed in the country—the College of Charleston and City College of New York. In the period roughly 1875-1925, nine others were chartered—Louisville, Hunter, Brooklyn, Cincinnati, Toledo, Akron, Detroit, Wichita, and Omaha.[7] The reasons assigned by those who were active in the establishing of these institutions showed great variety, but the chief ones were to keep young people under parental authority during their early college years; to provide a more practical education than that afforded by existing colleges; to provide better means of training teachers; to provide a center of culture for the city; and, in general, to meet specific local needs. This last reason became one of the most striking features of the work of these institutions. Their curricula and programs were geared to the specific needs of a given urban community.[8] As will be pointed out, this has special relevance for the evening college.

Outside college and university walls during this same fecund period from 1875 to 1925 there flourished almost innumerable forms of what may be called informal adult education—informal in the sense that it had nothing to do with credits, degrees, and the more formalized structure of university education. Yet it would be difficult to overestimate the cumulative effects on America in the years immediately preceding the day of radio, television, and the cinema. All over the land people gathered in Chautauqua tents to listen to Swiss bell ringers, band concerts, and noted lecturers. In the winter months the lyceum bureaus furnished sopranos who regaled their schoolhouse audiences with singing from classical music and lecturers who showed slides of faraway places. Libraries organized reading clubs and sponsored discussion groups. The YMCA promoted health and recreational programs, along with its religious activities and its evening classes. In 1889 the General Federation of Women's Clubs was formed as a result of the urge toward culture on the part of middle-class women over the country. In the cities such institutions as Cooper Union provided education for adults in many fields, particularly in "Americanization" courses for the foreign-born and even courses in reading and writing the English language. Popular magazines, such as *McClure's, Cosmopolitan, Forums, Everybody's,* and *Pearson's,* with their muckraking articles by such writers as Ida M. Tarbell and Lincoln Steffens, became standard fare in thousands of homes. In those that really went in for culture, President Charles W. Eliot's set called the Harvard Classics was likely to occupy a conspicuous section of the bookcase.

There was, of course, much dilettantism in all this, and many of the seeds of intellectualism were cast on barren and stony ground, but there were solid achievements as well. For all who believed in the processes of democracy it was significant that the gulf which separated the common man from the intellectuals was narrowed. Above all, it tended to prepare the soil for larger and better programs when they came along. One can see these influences in the extension movement, in the urge to found municipal universities, and finally in the evening college itself. It was in itself significant enough that the greatly beloved Lord Bryce could write of America: "The average of knowledge is higher, the habit of reading and thinking more generally diffused, than in any other country."[9]

Into this background one may fit the development of the evening college.

When the renaissance of the extension movement came after World War I, presidents of universities in urban areas found that the rapid urbanization of America had produced a situation where it was no longer desirable or necessary for them to go out into the highways and hedges to establish classes.[10] The demand existed right at their own doors. They had but to open the facilities of their universities evenings and Saturdays, to create the evening division. As has been pointed out above, many cities lacking any sort of facilities for higher education created municipal universities. Universities located in urban areas, instead, established the evening college, thus creating a fissure between extension education and residential education.[11] As time has passed, the fissure has grown. The tendency of the evening college has been to swing rather rapidly toward the pattern already established by the day colleges, to attempt to achieve respectability through academic orthodoxy. The extension movement has remained largely rural and small town except where in some states there has been established a network of extension centers in urban areas, which centers have in reality become evening colleges. An excellent example of the trend may be seen by examining the course of action taken by three pioneering institutions—Johns Hopkins, Chicago, and Wisconsin. Both Hopkins and Chicago (urban areas) have virtually abandoned extension work and have concentrated their efforts in evening colleges, McCoy College for the first named and University College for the second. The University of Wisconsin, not being located in a large urban area, has continued to expand its rural extension offerings but has set up residential centers in populous cities, Milwaukee for example.

Thus, it may be seen that the evening college is an urban phenomenon. It came into being as a result of the demands of urban people for educational facilities offered at a time when they could take advantage of them, and of the demands of industry and business for specialized training for their employees.[12] The need of the institutions for additional revenue was also a factor. Its development was over a period of time roughly corresponding to the development of the extension movement. Only seven of the fifty-five largest evening colleges were established before 1900. Forty-one were established between 1900 and 1929. The balance came after 1929. It is not surprising, too, that the privately endowed and the denominational college or university should largely be the home of the evening college, for they are urban institutions by and large while the state universities are not.[13]

By 1915 the problems and programs of the urban universities had become sufficiently differentiated from those of the state university to warrant the establishment of organizations of their own. A conference was called by the Commissioner of Education in Washington on November 9, 1914. By the fall of 1915 the Association of Urban Universities was functioning.[14] Each year at its annual meetings the problems of the urban university were discussed, and in these discussions adult education came in for its share of time. As a matter of fact, as the years went on the annual meetings might well have been mistaken for meetings of evening college deans, for they were the men who, by and large, were representing their universities instead of the presidents. This was far from what the founders of the Association had in mind. They had envisioned a small, fraternal association of college presidents in which *all* the problems of the urban university might be discussed, not merely the problems of the evening divisions.

At a meeting of the Association at the Hotel New Yorker in 1939 the leaders decided to revert to first principles and virtually to require that institutions be represented by their presidents instead of the evening college deans. The latter, sensing that their virtual domination of the Association was about to come to an end, met informally over coffee and decided that the time had come to form an organization of their own. The result was the Association of University Evening Colleges. The first president was Vincent H. Drufner of the University of Cincinnati.[15]

Although the evening college group may have been a bit piqued, actually there seems to have been little bitterness engendered over the break. For several years the two groups met concurrently and then drifted away from each other by selecting separate meeting places and times. It is profitless to argue who seceded from whom, as profitless as old men trying to decide whether they have given up sin or sin has given them up. Each side thought it was following its own line of interest. The separation could also be taken as a tacit recognition of the fact that evening college education was attaining a personality of its own. Unfortunately, however, the schism meant a loss of communication between the two groups who had many common problems which they must now discuss separately. One who has attended meetings of both is aware of the losses in understanding brought about by each going his own way.

The formation of the Association of University Evening

Colleges marks the second phase of the development of evening college education. It is a phase in which evening colleges became more articulate and conscious of their own identities. It was a period marked by enormous physical growth, for it includes the years when the G.I.'s came home and flocked into the evening divisions everywhere. In previous years its population growth had been slow and steady. Between 1945 and 1950 enrollment doubled. At the annual meetings of the Association deans and directors gathered to discuss their common problems, problems most often associated with physical growth. "How do you do it?" was the theme—how do you register students, how do you plan promotion and advertising campaigns, how do you handle veterans, how do you hire faculty members, how do you get along with the day colleges, how do you plan a conference or short course, what does the university do with the money you make, and a hundred other administrative questions. Occasionally someone slipped in a paper on the purpose of the evening college which questioned what all this activity was about educationally. It was listened to with great politeness, and then the deans and directors would return to their administrative problems.

One does not have to probe very deeply to discover the reasons for the state of mind which produced this condition. Virtually none of the deans and directors had had any specific training in the administration of evening colleges. Students were thronging into the halls for classes. Classes had to be provided, faculties hired, procedures of all sorts instituted; decisions had to be made on the spur of the moment in many cases. The dean was literally swamped with details, and for the management of them there was no rich background of experience and precedent upon which he could draw. If one is hacking his way through a jungle it is important, of course, to know where one is going; but it is also important to spend a great deal of time keeping one's machete sharpened, boots in repair, and a comfortable camp established at the end of the day. In short, housekeeping may be a chore but it is a necessary chore if goals are to be accomplished. One director wrote an educator prominent in the field of adult education a long letter describing all his administrative chores before registration and then: "while registration is going on the University budget man is breathing down my neck checking frequently on how our enrollment compares with the same day a year ago. . . . Damn it, Cy, how can a Director find time to think?"[16]

There did emerge from this period, however, a fairly coherent plan of administration which in spite of numerous important exceptions became relatively uniform in most of the larger evening colleges. Instead of giving this in a series of statistical tables the author chooses to ask and answer a series of questions on administration which it is hoped will make the pattern clear.[17]

What is the line of responsibility of evening college deans? They have one of two—either to the university head or some top university official, such as the dean of faculties or to the dean or deans of day colleges. In most of the large evening colleges the dean has a line of responsibility directly to the president. Many of the smaller college directors are responsible to a dean.

Who may enroll in an evening college? There is practically 100-percent agreement on the answer to this question. Any mature adult who has a desire to learn and who is educable may enroll in some phase or other of the evening division. Students who enroll to work toward degrees must fulfill the same entrance requirements as the day college student. Adults wishing to take special courses without degree credit may enroll without having completed high school. Most of the evening colleges have two classifications for students—"regular" and "special," or similar terms.

Who has control of degree programs? In the main, control over evening college undergraduate degree programs either is vested in one or more day colleges, or the day college has veto powers. Only 12 percent of evening colleges are the sole judges of their degree requirements.

Who approves new courses? Sixty-nine percent of the evening colleges report that evening credit courses must be approved by a day division committee. For noncredit courses the reverse is true; few day faculty committees concern themselves with noncredit courses. Evening divisions work closely with day departmental chairmen. In only 4 percent of the evening divisions is there no contact at all between them and day departmental chairmen. In 30 percent, departmental chairmen exercise only advisory power; in 33 percent, day chairmen have only partial administrative responsibility; in 33 percent, day chairmen have full administrative responsibility for evening college courses in their fields.

Who makes the budget? In 77 percent of the cases the evening college dean makes his own budget and submits it to the proper fiscal officer of the university. Twenty-three percent (again the smaller colleges) do not have a separate budget.

Where does the money which evening colleges make go? Forty-four percent report they are charged costs of operation other than instructional and administrative expense. In most evening divisions any excess of income over expenditures is credited to the general funds of the institution at the end of the year. Only 11 percent report that an excess of income over expenses for any given year may be carried over into the next.

Do evening colleges make money? Ninety-six percent report that year in and year out their income is greater than their expenditures. The amounts seem to depend upon the size of the college and upon the way individual university auditors figure "profit."

How much is tuition? Institutions may be divided in terms of tuition into two main categories—tax-supported schools and privately supported schools. In tax-supported schools undergraduate tuition may vary from no charge at all to $10 per credit hour. In the privately supported schools the fees begin at $10 per credit hour and go as high as $25. The average is somewhere around $14 to $15 per credit hour. This would make an ordinary three-hour course cost the student $42 to $45. Gradually increasing inflation which has increased costs of college operation has forced 66 percent of the evening colleges to raise fees within the past three years. Evening college deans are about evenly divided in their opinions of whether tuition fees have reached a point beyond which additional increases would cause a drop in enrollment.

Are scholarships and loans available to evening school students? Endowed scholarships are very rare in the evening college. However, financial assistance in the form of loans is on the increase. Eighty-six percent of the evening colleges grant loans or credit. In 38 percent of the institutions loans amount to less than 5 percent of the enrollment, but in 28 percent, loans are granted to from one fifth to one half of the students enrolled.

Are admission requirements in evening colleges the same as in the day colleges? Sixty-five percent have requirements identical with those of the day college. Thirty-five percent have different requirements.

Is the credit load of the evening student limited? The credit hour limit for evening students is largely an individual matter for each student. His scholastic ability, the nature of his employment and personal life, the nature of his motivation—all these bear in various degrees on the number of credit hours he can carry. However, 79 percent of the evening colleges have some limit. Of these, 35 percent limit the credit load to from six to eight hours; 54 percent place a limit of from nine to twelve hours; the balance apparently permit unlimited loads.

How are faculty members recruited? A very few evening colleges have a full-time faculty which teaches only in the evening division. A few more have a core faculty which teaches full time in the evening and to which is added the efforts of day faculty members and those recruited from the outside. Approximately 37 percent have no permanent faculty and depend entirely on day college faculty members and those recruited from the outside. There is a growing tendency in many institutions, however, to add new faculty members for a part of their teaching load in a day college and a part in the evening—a dual appointment arrangement.

What types of programs are offered in evening colleges? The answer to this, of course, is to go back to the classification made at the beginning of this chapter. The noncredit institutions offer only nondegree programs; those giving credit have a variety of programs, including noncredit. Perhaps expanding the original classification a bit will make clear the type of offerings.

In the multidimensional classification any one of three types of programs may be selected by the student—a degree program, a certificate program, or a noncredit program. In this classification the two most common degrees are the bachelor of arts and the bachelor of commerce. Certificate programs are designed for the student who may wish to work toward a specific goal but who does not desire a degree. Ordinarily the requirements for the certificate are roughly those of the junior college. Nondegree programs are of two varieties. In one a student may sit in on any course he wishes but take no examinations and receive no credits. This is ordinarily referred to as "auditing" a course. In the other he may take special adult noncredit courses designed specifically for those who wish to improve themselves but who do not wish to put in as many class hours as would be required in auditing a course.

In the other classifications—technical, commercial, and liberal arts—the same general plan applies with variations. The noncredit type of institution, as has been suggested, is much freer to offer a wide variety of courses which ordinarily would not appear in a credit or degree program.

These questions of administration, faculty, budget, curricula, lines of authority—in general, the relationship of the evening college to the rest of the university—constitute an important group of problems with which evening college deans have been wrestling. That the day and evening divisions appear to have reached some sort of rough pattern of *rapprochement* does not mean that all evening colleges are happy with the outcome; nor, indeed, are all the day colleges. Perhaps the present situation is only a truce, or even a stalemate. It is obvious, however, that many of the older deans are now turning one eye at least from these problems to a consideration of larger problems—the problems or roles, of a philosophical rationale for what they are doing, reasons for their existence. This new approach to larger problems of the evening college marks another epoch in its development. It might well be said that evening college education is in a process of transition from the how-we-do-it phase to the why-we-do-it. Caution should be exercised, however, in accepting this too literally or too fully. Many of the deans, particularly those who are developing new evening colleges, are still very much in the first stage. Too, some older deans have been unable to separate their thinking from the excruciating minutiae of administrative problems so that they may maturely reflect on larger considerations. Care should be exercised also in thinking that because a sort of administrative stalemate has been achieved, thereby the administrative problems of the evening college have been settled. Such is far from true. As will be pointed out in later chapters, the status quo is an uneasy one for the evening college in many respects.

This present phase of evening college education which is characterized by an approach to mature thinking may be said, in a very real sense, to date from the founding of the Center for the Study of Liberal Education for Adults in 1951. This small, closely knit, highly articulate group of young scholars was brought into existence through the efforts of certain leaders in the Association of University Evening Colleges and is financed by the Fund for Adult Education. It has as its purpose "providing aid and leadership to the persons, ideas, and programs that can help develop the evening college into a more effective instrument for the liberal education of adults." Its program is divided into three major areas of activity: (1) the improvement of curriculum materials, with emphasis on developing experimental discussion guides; (2) the development of leadership for *university level* adult education; and (3) co-ordination and communication within evening colleges, between evening colleges, and between evening colleges and nonacademic agencies of adult education.[18]

The Center has done a lot of things. It has conducted research, published papers by members of its own staff, published papers by other people who are thinking about evening college education, held workshops and conferences of various types and on various subjects, developed new curriculum materials, and engaged in a host of other activities. These are all, however, means to an end, devices to stimulate thinking, for the Center is more thought-oriented than action-oriented. In the author's opinion the most noteworthy contribution it has made is the questions it has raised—questions which sooner or later must be answered if the evening college is to be meaningful in our society. "What is the role of the evening college in our society?" it has asked. "What is the role of the urban university in its community?" "Are existing academic attitudes and practices appropriate for university adult education?" "What is the purpose of noncredit adult programs?" "Can the liberal arts be merchandised?" "What do we mean by liberal education?" "What should be the relationship of the evening college to the rest of the university?" "What should the evening college do for the individual?" "How can we best train leaders in evening college education?" "How can we improve instruction?"

These and scores of other questions have been raised by the Center. Some of them, at least, are not new, but these young scholars have reshaped them and resharpened them and then have patiently, unobtrusively, but provocatively, demanded answers, or at least thinking in the direction of answers. Not only this, but through workshops and publications a forum has been provided wherein these questions may be debated. When we consider the fact that some leaders in the field already were asking some of these questions, it is small wonder that evening college education is today so encouragingly introspective. In fact, there is no segment of higher education in America today which is seeking more diligently or more intelligently the answers to its problems than evening college education.

With this in mind it might be well to indicate some of the major facets or dimensions of evening college education as they exist at the present time.

The evening college is not, as some have been unkind enough to suggest, an illegitimate child. It is legitimate, but it was born at a time when the parents were old and set in their ways. The parents were sorely puzzled over how to handle this precocious and, at times, somewhat erratic youngster. There was the sharp and gnawing fear that the child might disgrace the family, so there was plotted a course of action which would make it conform to the behavior pattern established for the other children. The child, being young and somewhat insecure over the lack of parental affection, submitted, but not without some resulting trauma. When the family was seated around the table and the well-meaning father was helping the plates, Junior found his was often not heaped so high as the others. In fact, there were times when it was made quite clear to the child that he had best make plans to secure his own food because most of what was available probably would be needed for the other members of the family. At the table, too, he found the other children looking somewhat askance at him. It is small wonder, then, that this youngest child of the university should develop a defensive attitude which in overt behavior might take any one of several forms—self-pity, belligerency, boastfulness, frustration, or any combination of these.

In its present stage of more mature thinking many of the evening colleges are turning the light on these neuroses and psychosomatic tensions through intelligent discussion and planning. They are beginning to feel the necessity for working out with the rest of the academic family their proper place in the scheme of things. They are also beginning to find out that they must themselves understand their role or roles in the total picture of university education; that no traveler is so bewildered as he who is uncertain about where he wants to go. In fact, if they could encounter an equally liberal, enlightened, and conscientious attitude on the part of many of their brothers, the answer would come easier.

Another facet or dimension which is coming sharply into focus is the trimodal nature of the demands made upon the evening college. These may be enumerated as the demands of the individual, of the community, and of the academic tradition. These are not always mutually exclusive, but they often present apparent contradictions as some voices cry, "Go this way," and others cry, "Go that way." There are areas of thought in adult education which are coming to be almost cultish in their nature. One group holds that attention should be focused on the worth of the individual and on his social and educational needs to the exclusion of any serious consideration of the action-oriented community-centered group education. On the other hand, the exponents of this latter phase insist that adult education takes place in community action groups but that our colleges stand apart from the community; that the need of adult education is not for information but experience in group work; and that the adult education field needs leaders instead of teachers. And while leaders of these two groups speak their lines on the stage, the guardian of the academic tradition stands in the wings and constantly warns that academic respectability and high standards must be maintained if either side is to amount to anything.

The evening college dean and faculty ordinarily are unwilling to take an extreme position because there is the slowly dawning realization that perhaps both groups have more in common than they are willing to admit; that the evening college must do a great deal for both the individual and the community. This academic agility has never been better explained than by Cyril O. Houle at the 1953 meeting of the Association of University Evening Colleges in St. Louis. The evening college, he said, "cannot escape the necessity of deriving its purposes from a consideration of all three of these factors—the individual, the community, and the academic tradition." The evening college, he continued, "is like the great dams of the TVA which must be administered with several objectives in mind, all of them compelling and some of them contradictory. For purposes of power, as much water as possible must be kept in the reservoirs so that it will be available for future use in case of drought. For purposes of flood control, as little water as possible must be kept in the reservoirs so there will be a place to store flood waters. For purposes of malaria control, there must be a periodic raising and lowering of the water in the reservoir so that the larvae which live in the shallow water may be stranded on the sand and die. For purposes of navigation, there must always be a nine-foot channel so that ships may make their unimpeded way to the high hills of Tennessee. The engineer who controls the system of dams must be aware of all these aspects, each with its articulate proponents. As the year progresses, and rain and drought succeed one another, he must make an infinitely varied series of calculations, taking into account both continuing demands and the immediate situation. He can not choose conservation, or flood control, or navigation as his ultimate end; he must strike a balance among them. The evening college dean is in the same situation. If he takes the academic tradition, the individual, or the community as his final goal and subordinates the other to it, he will have a result which differs in each case in terms of the goal which he has made paramount but which will always be unhappy and will usually destroy the essence of the evening college."[20]

One might go on almost endlessly citing examples of this healthy intellectual ferment which characterizes evening college education as it hovers between youth and early maturity, but these must suffice. Encouraging as all this thinking is, however, there must be mentioned its most serious defect. *It is largely unilateral.* The evening college dean each year attends a number of conferences, workshops, and the meeting of his Association. In between times he reads and even thinks. He becomes convinced of the righteousness of his cause and at times receives great illuminations on purposes and roles. But here the matter rests. Not enough of it gets through to the day deans, day faculty members, the president, or the board of trustees. As a result there is no meeting of minds on the problems of evening college education. Attractive and promising as this present flowering may be, it must be cross-pollinated by the thinking of others in the university outside the evening college if it is to bear mature fruit.

A good example of the lack of homogenized thinking

among various segments of the university is the matter of the institution's relation to its immediate community. The evening college dean and faculty are likely to place great emphasis upon the community aspects of adult education: to insist that the university pursue an ever broadening policy of extending its services to many segments of the community which in the past have not been counted as the concern of higher education. On the other hand, many day college deans and faculties (and even presidents) look with jaundiced eyes upon any project which would take the institution out of its customary role of providing educational opportunities for a select few within a certain age group.

The fact that there is no meeting of minds on this most important topic of the university's relation to the community makes it desirable that at least an approach to the matter be made.

3 The Evening College and the Community

BEFORE commenting on the relationship of the evening college to its community it might be well to note the difference between the strictly urban university (the municipal university) and the university in an urban area. The former, as has been pointed out, is a tax-supported institution with its clientele, at least in theory, restricted almost wholly to the immediate community which surrounds it. The university in an urban area, on the other hand, is likely to be a denominational or privately endowed university which faces in two directions—toward its immediate community and toward a region or, indeed, a nation. These facts may make a great deal of difference in community relationships. The former is, or should be, able to concentrate on programs designed specifically for the metropolitan area and its peculiar needs; the latter must divide its efforts. Unless otherwise specified, this chapter deals with the university in an urban area and the problems it faces in carrying out a program geared to the needs of its immediate community without at the same time penalizing its programs intended to satisfy the needs of a much larger area, which needs may differ radically from those of its home community. (By home community is meant the urban areas immediately surrounding a university in which students may commute by ordinary means of transportation.)

With the rapid urbanization of this country, urban universities are faced with the necessity of considerable soul searching regarding their educational commitments. Historic obligations and commitments made when the university lived in a simpler age may still be binding, but new ones press for solutions, and the administration is faced with the decisions. What are the obligations of the university to the home community? In the face of rising educational costs can the university afford to make an all-out commitment to the educational needs of adults in the community? On the other hand, can it afford not to?

There are three possible answers which the university can make: First, there would be the answer that the urban university has no obligations beyond those historic ones to students who can afford to attend school full time in the daytime. Second, there could be the reply that the university has a deep obligation to the adult educational needs of the community and that this commitment must be accepted as of equal importance with its historic obligations to students in the day colleges; that wherever and whenever necessary, funds out of university endowment income will be dedicated to the purposes of adult education. The third response is a compromise such as was implicit in the case of the Oriental potentate who conferred on the British ambassador's wife the Order of Chastity, Second Class. This third reply admits a serious obligation to the adult education needs of the community and would say that steps should be taken to implement the obligation, provided university funds needed for other educational activities are not required.

At the present time most of the evening college adult education activities of our urban universities probably operate under the philosophy of answer number three. There is hardly a university president or board of trustees which does not today at least pay lip service to the cause of university level adult education, and many of them are genuinely sincere in their belief that the university ought to direct a large share of attention in that direction. In the face of slowly increasing endowment funds and rapidly rising costs of operation, however, they are unwilling to make an all-out new financial commitment. The evening college must finance itself, and, if possible, make a substantial contribution to the general income of the university. One university president summed up the matter very succinctly and very honestly somewhat as follows: "We think we have a good evening college and we are glad to render what we consider a real service to the community. I would be less than honest, however, if I did not say that both the board and I look with some misgivings at taking on a new educational venture of this magnitude unless it can pay its own way. We are an old university but we are not wealthy. We have long-established obligations to the students in our liberal arts college and in our professional schools. We are struggling to provide the necessary finances so that those obligations can be met. Somewhere along the line we must limit ourselves to the size job we can do. With our present university endowment we must establish a cut-off point somewhere. At present I could not say where that would be. Certainly we would not wish to discontinue our evening division, but if ever it came to a point where it cut substantially into our endowment income and imperiled other colleges I think the board would consider such a step."

One suspects that if the country's college and university presidents were polled this would fairly well express their sentiments. It has the dubious virtue of pragmatism to commend it; but upon a close examination it not only begs the question but reveals a value system which puts a precariously narrow base under higher education. It says essentially that a value system is in effect which gives priority to the education of young people who can attend school during the day and who can afford the time and money required for a four-year program; that although this is a minority group it has historically been the group upon which our educational institutions have concentrated their efforts and thus should continue to be favored even though changing times and conditions should push to the front new groups equally intelligent and equally needful of an education. If this system of values were measured entirely in terms of the needs of society, it would quickly break down, for it appears extremely doubtful if we can afford to have in our national life a great mass of poorly educated young adults. Perhaps some university will startle the country one day by launching an endowment drive aimed at raising money which will put the university in a position to afford every worthy person in the community an education. Such would have a powerful appeal and would have as its philosophy something like this: "The university must continue to serve the basic needs of those who can come to us for full-time college work. But we must also make it possible for every qualified man and woman in this community regardless of age or occupation to continue his education. Only in this way can we build the good community."

The preceding paragraphs may seem to imply that the evening college is the only agency of the urban university concerned with the community. Such, of course, is not true. If the university had no evening college, it still would serve its immediate community in almost countless important ways. It trains teachers for the city schools; it furnishes business executives, doctors, lawyers, social workers, engineers, and journalists. Its consultant and research facilities are invaluable. Its faculty contributes of its time and talent to community projects. It brings to its campus desirable people, both students and faculty, who are cultural assets and who, the chamber of commerce might add, may spend as much money annually in the city as the employees of a good-sized industry. Its football games (if it has a good team) bring visitors into the city nearly every Saturday during the fall, and they spend considerable sums of money at hotels, restaurants, and bars, to say nothing of entertaining the home folk. In short, it's a mighty good thing, the civic clubs would say, for a city to have a university in it—good culturally and economically.

On close examination, however, it is clear that these services are actually almost incidental—that is, they are services which the university renders by the very fact that it is in the community. If its administration never gave one second's thought to the problem of how an urban university should serve its local community, these services probably would go right on. With the insistent demands of modern urban life, however, it seems quite likely that elementary questions of survival will eventually require that a university think through the question of what its *total* obligation to its community is.

This is, of course, a basic question which each university must answer for itself, for no two urban communities have identical problems. It is quite likely, however, that every urban institution will discover very early in its process of thinking out the answers that it does have the dual nature mentioned above and that its day programs do not satisfy the total needs of the community. The realization then comes that there must be in the university some college or division whose program is geared directly to the needs and demands of the immediate community. This is, to a large extent, the evening division, for there are certain functions which only it can perform because of its proximity to large segments of the adult population.

Let us assume that a university has decided to face the basic issues. It has determined what its total obligations to the community are and has assigned to the evening college its part of a co-ordinated program. What then?

The first and most obvious answer is that most evening colleges would be embarrassed by their inability to fulfill their assigned role. This is true because of the lack of knowledge of techniques for determining what the really basic needs of the community are, a condition often shared by day and evening divisions alike. A community is not a simple social organism. It is a vastly complex structure, and one does not really know it merely by living in it for a period of years. Below the surface of the tossing sea of humanity which we call a city there lie hidden shoals as well as hidden treasures for the educator. By sailing uncharted waters the evening college dean is likely to encounter more shoals than treasures.

Or, the approach to community problems by many day and evening divisions may be likened to that of an inexperienced quail hunter. The dog flushes a covey of quail. There they are, a whirring blur of feathers. The neophyte blazes away at the covey, but ordinarily he doesn't hit anything. As every hunter knows, a man must pick individual birds out of the covey and shoot them down. Otherwise, he will make a big noise but go home with an empty bag.

Actually, this is too often the case in dealing with community needs. There is the great noise of blasting away at the whole community, but results are often negligible. All of which is a way of saying that the community must become the subject of the most intensive investigation and study if one wishes to construct programs which will satisfy its wants and needs. One must select those problem areas to which he wishes to devote attention and then concentrate upon them.

The study of the community is not an easy thing, but there is general information available which should be of substantial assistance to the evening college dean and faculty. The sociology department of the university usually has one or more faculty members who devote special attention to urban problems. Most of these are available for consultation. There is an approach, however, which seems worthy of particular note, an approach suggested by Professor Gordon Blackwell of the University of North Carolina.[1]

This plan Mr. Blackwell has characterized as "a kind of highway map for us in exploring the community sociologically." It is composed of seven "guide lines as dimensions of community" in its *static* state of existence. These are:

1. *The population base.* Obviously this involves the necessity of knowing something about the raw material that

makes up the community. Who are the people? What is their age and sex composition? What are the racial characteristics of the population, the nationality groups, the educational level of the people, their mobility within the city? What about population origins and migration (rural, foreign, etc.)? Obviously this has profound implications for any institution really interested in a good job of adult education at any level.

2. *The institutional structure.* This, of course, means the complex web of formally organized social relationships which people have created in order to help them better to meet their needs. There is the family, of course, which is basic. There are such institutions as churches, schools, hospitals, social welfare agencies, business and industry, newspapers, radio and television, labor unions, civic clubs, the chamber of commerce, the PTA, and scores of others, of which the evening college must be aware in planning programs.

3. *Value systems.* Included in this category are those value systems which have a high priority with a community. How does the community feel about government, or moral codes, or hospitality, or education, or any one of a score of other factors which have social significance?

4. *Social stratification.* This means, of course, the way all communities have of layering people according to range and prestige, large groups of unorganized people being ranged as higher or lower than other similarly unorganized groups. The social class is the inevitable result of such stratification, and a knowledge of class and caste is absolutely necessary to the individual who plans an adult education program in the community.

5. *Informal social relationships.* This is quite a different

factor from organized social relationships and not nearly so easy to define. Perhaps it can best be described as a sort of informal community network of people and groups who are important as opinion leaders and formers. Actually it is a sort of interpersonal relationship of people who are important not for their wealth or power but for their ability to influence other people. It represents a sort of power structure of the influential instead of a power structure of the mighty. Every community has this network, and the wise evening college dean will make use of it.

6. *The power structure.* This factor is somewhat related to the informal social relationship item mentioned above in that it, too, is an interpersonal, unorganized network based on power. Who are the men in a given community who by virtue of their wealth and power put across or veto a community project? Find these men, and one has the power structure.[2]

7. *The ecology.* Included in this would be those factors of the spatial distribution of people and the way the people have been divided up in terms of social and economic functions. Where do people live? What kind of people live where? How do they make a living? What are their traffic and transportation problems? Are there migratory trends apparent? These are typical ecological problems which have great relevance for the university interested in developing a community education program.

It is perfectly apparent that Blackwell's road map is a very broad one. It, as he freely admits, takes into consideration little of the dynamic nature of the community. Neither does it attempt to get off the broad highways into the intricate smaller roads which one must know if the terrain is to be completely familiar. It is necessary in investigating the community to become thoroughly familiar with the little country roads which lead into Blackwell's seven highways. A very interesting approach to this is furnished by Robert J. Havighurst of the University of Chicago.[3] Havighurst has taken a segment from the community population dimension and has subjected it to the closest study. This population segment is the middle-aged group. Middle age, he says, is *terra incognita*. We know a great deal about childhood, adolescence, and even old age—but knowledge of middle age is limited to a small amount of specialized knowledge gained from psychiatrists, social workers, and marriage counselors. Middle age is the summer of life, he says. How does it differ from spring and autumn?

In answering, Havighurst has constructed a social role theory for middle age. Social roles are, he says, "activity-patterns that can be seen in more than one individual, and which many people commonly fill." The activities can be thought of as completely independent of the individual and fall into certain categories. These are:

Worker	Parent
Husband or wife	Homemaker or home member
Son or daughter	Citizen
Friend	Club or association member
User of leisure time	Member of a religious group

If a person's activities in these roles are defined, he feels, most of his life in the community will be defined. For example, what are the activities and interests and needs of the middle-aged parent? Are they the same as for the young parent? Or has his role as a worker changed over a period of twenty-five years? These and related questions have great relevance for the university which attempts to understand and serve the community. It is the individual bird rather than the covey technique.

It becomes instantly obvious how this same technique could be applied to segments of all the dimensions listed by Blackwell. For example, under this same dimension of population comes the term "educational levels," to which we may add "sources of information and opinions." It is inconceivable that any broad program of community education could be undertaken without adequate knowledge of the educational levels of various segments of the population. A knowledge of the media through which these segments receive information and form opinions would also be necessary. From this, one might proceed to break down and analyze segment after segment of the community until a fairly clear picture of the needs of people in a community might be drawn, a fact which indicates the enormous amount of investigation which must be carried on.

One of the virtues of the Havighurst hypothesis is that it sheds light on how community "needs" may be discovered. This word "needs" has been bandied about until it may have lost meaning. One group uses it so generically that it loses all semantic preciseness. Another group tries to dissect it so minutely that it is submerged in details. Somewhere between the general and the esoterically precise there is a working definition of community needs. Perhaps one might begin with a concept of a need not as being something but rather the *absence of something*. A need is the lack of anything requisite, desirable, or useful. A need is the gap between an actual condition and a norm or standard; or, to phrase it a bit differently, a need is the difference between what a condition is and what it ought to be.[4] Applying this to the Havighurst hypothesis, one role might be selected as an illustration—the citizen role, let us say. The middle-aged citizen group can never identify its needs unless it discovers in some way a desirable norm for good citizenship. A recognition of standards, therefore, becomes of paramount importance if a felt group need is to be the motivating factor in any sort of educational experience. This is not to say that a recognition of such a norm or standard will automatically assure that the citizen will be aroused to satisfy the needs which become apparent; it simply means that without the norm no need will emerge in a recognizable form.

It seems implicit in what Blackwell and Havighurst have said that some sort of rough classification of needs might be made somewhat as follows: (a) basic community-wide needs, (b) refined group needs, (c) individual needs.

By basic community-wide needs is meant those needs common to all groups, which no individual group can ignore. These would include, but not be limited to, sanitation, housing, education, crime prevention—in general, the maintenance of a physical environment in which survival and growth are possible. Above this comes a refinement of needs wherein groups because of cultural differences, age, or some other factor become separated from the mass and each group develops needs peculiar to itself. The variety of these needs is almost infinite and makes for extreme complexity when viewed by the university which has a willingness to interest itself in helping the group discover norms and satisfy needs. These are the groups which in spite of the trend toward the mass community make up the individual "publics" with which the urban university must deal.[5] Individual needs are, of course, those peculiar to the individual as he separates himself from the group.

Since both basic community-wide needs and individual needs will be touched upon later in this book, it seems desirable here to explore a bit further the category of refined group needs. Let us assume that a university is interested in formulating programs of value to women in the community. Immediately it appears that there are "publics" among women. One, therefore, might need to ask:

I. What are the roles or needs of elderly women?
    a. Those of some means who have retired and live in an apartment house and spend their time knitting and chatting with other women of their age?
    b. Those who still maintain homes but are widows?
    c. Those living with sons or daughters?
II. What are the roles or needs of middle-aged women?
    a. The housewife whose children are all married or otherwise away from the parental roof?
    b. The middle-aged widow who picks up a career late in life?
    c. The middle-aged businesswoman who has never married?
    d. The middle-aged widow without family responsibilities who has been left financially secure?
III. What are the roles or needs of the young woman?
    a. The young businesswoman without family responsibility?
    b. The young married woman who is combining marriage and a career?
    c. The young wife with children of preschool age?
    d. The young wife with children between six and fifteen?
    e. The young woman who is working until she can get married?

From this simple and incomplete illustration it is obvious that "needs" as applied to the generic term "women" in a community is so general as to be almost meaningless. It is only when the public of women is broken down into sub-publics that the term "community of women" comes to have any practical significance. One might go on with this sort of analysis; in fact, the evening college dean must go on with it in many other areas if his programs are to be designed to meet real rather than imaginary community needs. And it is precisely at this point that the problem becomes so difficult.

Many of these problems and challenges of a community-oriented adult education program are illustrated by the experimental efforts of one evening college dean. Having been given a relatively free hand by the university administration but lacking the financial resources to carry out investigation as ambitious and thorough as the Blackwell-Havighurst plan, he decided to make a start by utilizing whatever existing data there might be on his community. In his preliminary and almost random searches for data he found that the university department of sociology had only recently completed a very thorough population study of the immediate urban areas. The city had been divided into zones, and population characteristics of each had been most carefully studied and recorded. Educational levels, income brackets, age ranges, national origins, occupations, and many other factors were studied. The data had then been transferred to a series of charts so that it was comparatively easy to get a comprehensive picture of population characteristics.

As an experimental approach the dean decided to determine how many of these areas or zones were being served directly by the university. He secured an enormous map of the city and placed it on his office wall. Enrollment records for a considerable period of time were utilized to determine the residence areas of the people who had in any way been served by some division of the university. Not much to his surprise he found many areas where the university was making no direct impression whatever. These showed up as great barren spaces in the forest of pins which denoted people who had been served.

"What are these areas like?" he asked himself, and then decided he would try to find out. From the population study he found several facts which had implications for the adult educator: there was a high percentage of functional illiteracy; the areas were populated by native whites, native Negroes, and first and second-generation foreigners; they were predominately semiskilled and nonskilled workers with low incomes. From visits to the areas he further learned that a large percentage of both native whites and Negroes had only recently moved into the city from surrounding rural areas. After deciding to concentrate on this group, he pushed his studies a bit further. Housing was found to be deplorable. Practically none of the people had voted. They didn't know how to register nor where the polling places were. It was rare to find one who was availing himself of the recreational facilities which the city provided. The men were spending their evenings in near-by juke joints drinking beer, and the women just stayed home. Most of the families possessed a radio, but virtually none read the daily newspapers regularly. Very few of the women interviewed had any knowledge of nutrition and of how to utilize a limited income to provide a balanced diet for a family.

Back in his office the dean pondered what he had discovered. Then to him came the puzzling questions which come to every university adult educator similarly confronted. Is this the sort of thing with which a university ought to concern itself? was his first thought. Is it any of our business? Aren't we in the business of administering higher education to students who come to us on our campus? Aren't there other agencies which should deal with these problems?

It so happened that this particular evening college dean did think these matters were of concern to a university, for he felt that a great educational institution, even though it might not be able to do the job directly, ought to assume the leadership in formulating programs to supply crying needs which had been discovered in the community. In this particular case he confronted the board of education with the almost unbelievable extent of functional illiteracy in certain areas, and the board shifted its adult program to care for the situation. He alerted the League of Women Voters to the nonvoting habits of these people, and the League organized a program designed especially for them. When the city recreational department was made to realize how little its program meant to hundreds of these people, a campaign of education was launched designed to draw them into healthy recreational activities.

It should be noted that in no one of these cases did the university through its evening college directly administer a program to fill a community need. It merely supplied the leadership and assistance for other community educational or quasi-educational agencies who actually did the job.

There are other types of needs and problems at other levels which the university can best attack directly. For example, another evening college dean in another city discovered that a group of suburban housewives were hungry for information on foreign affairs which would enable them to read the newspapers more intelligently. Most of them were college graduates, and none wanted college credit. Here clearly was a type of need which the university should itself undertake to fill. It did so by organizing at the branch library in this suburban area a noncredit course called "The World Today," led by a faculty member who was not only qualified as an expert in the field of international relations, but who had an interest in community affairs.

It would appear, therefore, that the ideal position for an evening college to take would be one in which both phases, "higher" education and community service, would be looked upon as important. The tendency is for many evening colleges to overlook the fact that one of their most important services could be that of supplying the imagination, the research, and the leadership for community educational groups anxious and willing to function if only they can be given guidance in conceptualizing needs.

The first dean mentioned above who made a minor safari into the problem jungles of his own community does not feel that any sort of sensational results were secured. The experience did, however, serve to point out for him the basic questions of policy and procedure which any university will have to face if it proposes to be really community-minded. Chiefly the questions are: Should the university:

a. Find its own phase of the community effort, try to develop that well, and let the balance go?

b. Survey community needs and make known the results to interested groups but exercise little or no supervision or guidance?

c. Attempt to harness the many separate efforts of various adult education groups into some semblance of a meaningful over-all pattern? An adult education council, for example?

d. Go in for social action programs?

e. Try only to train community adult education leaders?

f. Concentrate on training the individual student with the hope that he may become a socially conscious community leader and thus discharge the college's community obligations?

g. Help to determine community needs, make known the results to interested groups, and then give every possible assistance to those who are willing to undertake social action programs?

It is obvious that a particular institution will answer these questions in the light of what sort of institution it conceives itself to be. Universities do have different concepts of their roles in the community. One has its roots in the idea that the day programs more or less as they stand are desirable for adults. Proponents of this idea in effect say: Our society does not make it possible for all young people to get a college education in the four years immediately following high school; we will offer it to them in whatever time is free after the day's work is done; we will provide the facilities, as much like those of the day colleges as possible, and we will reward effort by giving credits and awarding degrees just as the day colleges do. In short, we will lengthen the school day from 8:00 A.M. to 3:00 P.M. to 8:00 A.M. to 10:00 P.M. Ours, they say, will be strictly a day college frame of reference.

Another concept relates the evening college directly to the adult education movement. This concept would reject almost entirely the day frame of reference and substitute for it one grounded in community needs regardless of credit or degrees. Short courses, noncredit lecture-discussion courses organized especially for adults, radio and television education, conferences, and workshops constitute the *pièce de résistance*. This concept would place upon the university evening college the responsibility of becoming a sort of center for adult education activities of whatever nature which have relevance for community needs.[6]

In between these two concepts are ranged various shades and combinations, with most institutions adopting some of both. Perhaps no better way to make concepts clear is afforded than the views of the deans and directors themselves.[7]

One dean sees dimly the need for a community-oriented program but feels the "obvious and primary purpose of a university evening college is to provide the same credit sequences, both graduate and undergraduate, that are available in the day sessions." He concedes that the evening college might "service specialized community needs" but feels that its real function is "to provide instruction in line with traditions of institutions of higher learning."

In a similar view another writes that in his evening college "we simply observe all of the academic standards set up by the academic authorities of the college. Each course is taught as a parallel course except for those modifications in techniques which every good adult teacher must adopt." And joining in this sentiment is still another who feels that adult education should consist of courses which have respectability when measured by the dictates of the academic tradition. Community service programs would be minimized because this is not traditionally a function of an institution of higher learning. "Adult education can best be served," he feels, "by the college in those areas in which it has experience and particular competence."

Still another dean, who obviously has wrestled with his own conscience as well as with the ideas of the academician, feels that "the consideration of evening college goals in terms of community needs and pressures can be discussed only within the limitations imposed by the university. In other words, if the evening college deals with credit courses and traditional academic programs, there are many community needs and interests which do not come within its scope." Furthermore, he feels, "no evening college should attempt to meet community needs which can be met better by other agencies, with the additional provision that the college may have unused resources, when the other agencies have exhausted theirs." The evening college in a community, he writes, "should serve as the capstone of the adult education programs in terms of training leaders and providing resources which other agencies cannot provide" but if "nontraditional" programs are to be offered they "should have a different name just as you differentiate between a resident college and an extension service."

"Just what should be our role in this particular type [community service, noncredit] of education?" asks another dean. His institution is, he states, "trying to assess our role in the total adult education program in the city," but he confesses confusion. There are so many other institutions in the city which provide adults with opportunities for further learning. (Perhaps this is most typical of the attitude of institutions not firmly wedded to the traditional types of higher education offered for those who have the necessary secondary school qualifications and can come to the campus.)

According to another dean the "real school for adults" should be one which discards entirely the credit-course concept and goes all out for the type of programs which fill community needs—any needs at any level.

Other interesting excerpts might be made from these letters, but the portions cited here pretty clearly reveal certain basic concepts of the leaders of evening college education. On the whole, it is a somewhat confused and hazy picture which emerges, but there are a few rather clear conclusions which are indicated: (1) There is no meeting of minds on what sort of program will best serve the community. The gamut is from those who would have no credit courses to those who doubt the value of noncredit courses. (2) There is a pronounced tendency to think of adult community education solely in terms of formal "courses." (3) A dichotomy exists between "adult education" and "education for adults." The former is adventitious, of doubtful respectability, and is thought of as being a sort of second-rate program of noncredit courses, while the latter is given a higher rating and is thought of as highly respectable, consisting of credit and degree courses. Obviously, most time and attention is devoted to the degree programs, probably because of the demands of the individual and the community for this sort of education. (4) Many recognize some kind of obligation to the community and are developing some sort of patchwork of noncredit courses, but no one has made a sufficiently intensive study of his community to know what needs he is trying to meet. (5) The academic tradition is largely, if not entirely, the controlling factor in all courses, both credit and noncredit.

As if enough questions without answers had not been raised already, still another must be considered: Assuming that a university has discovered what the needs of the community are, how can it get the citizenry to participate in programs aimed at meeting those needs? Or, to state the matter in other words, "research is still required to find out how far in the life of a community the awareness of needs is in itself a sufficient incentive for action by the citizenry, or what must be added so that awareness will lead to action."[8]

An individual feels hungry. This is a signal that he has or thinks he has a need for food. This is a basic, raw, individual need; but he may at the same time be suffering from a vitamin deficiency of which the doctor has reminded him from time to time but which he ignores because it is less imminently insistent and not so strongly felt. Similarly, a community may make demands that a crossing be made safe, that mosquitoes be eliminated, that a dusty street be paved, or that all dogs be vaccinated to eliminate rabies. These may come under the category of basic community-wide needs and they may be essential; but at the same time, the community may be suffering from cultural avitaminosis without taking any action on the malady whatever. How may the community, or certain community groups, be encouraged to support programs which are designed to supply the vitamin deficiency?

We might answer that question, "Nobody knows for sure," and thus end the matter; but there are some approaches and considerations which might be included in thinking about an answer.

One must know through what media and at what levels community groups receive the information upon which they form opinions. Let us assume that it is considered desirable for certain community groups to understand the ideals and functions of the United Nations. Would one organize a formal course of lectures, plan a series of film forums, promote a series of television shows or a radio series, resort to newspapers (if so, morning or evening?), or organize a series of small discussion groups in the neighborhood? Or shall there be a combination of these? Second, there must be careful planning of course content and of method of presentation. Content must be palatable as well as potent, and the teacher must bring to it all the skills of a group leader. Third, it will have a better chance of success if it has in it the elements of controversy and contemporaneousness. Fourth, it must be publicized or promoted so that all interested participants may know about it.

But having said all this, the evening college is faced with the probability that not more than half the courses carefully planned and adequately publicized will attract enough participants to warrant offering them. One case will illustrate this discouraging feature. A dean and instructor carefully planned a course on Korea shortly after our decision to intervene. The public to which the "pitch" was to be made was selected with great care. The instructor was a well-known authority in the field and had participated in numerous United Nations studies in Korea. Excellent promotional efforts went into the planning. It had the characteristic of contemporaneousness with the strong probability of controversy. The course was a natural. It had everything. That is, it had everything except participants. Only five people registered. At the same time a course in botany for the home gardener, not nearly so well planned or publicized, drew nearly two hundred registrants.

A puzzled dean tried to analyze the reasons for unexpected failure on the one hand and unexpected success on the other. Then suddenly out of mental perturbation came insight, and the reasons became perfectly clear. The air was full of Korea. One had only to relax in the comfort of his own living room and listen on radio or look and listen to television to hear world authorities discuss the problem. Commentators by the dozen provided controversy. The newspapers provided news and editorial comment. The weekly news magazines were full of it. Why should anyone give up an evening and pay out money for tuition when he could get as good or better at home? On the other hand, the air was not full of botany for the home gardener. The only way the home gardener could get the information he felt he needed was by giving up an evening, paying tuition, and going to the university. The course, too, had the virtue of being directed solely at gardening problems in the immediate locality.

It may well be that the general informational or cultural courses are on their way to join the linen duster and the Chautauqua in limbo. They disappeared as conditions changed—served their purposes well and then gave way before the closed car and the appearance of new media of mass information and entertainment. The newest and most powerful of these new media is, of course, television—a medium which eventually may supplant many of the more formal courses offered on the university campus and intended for community consumption. There are many things to recommend it: it reaches people in their homes when they are in a receptive mood; it reaches more people than can be reached via the classroom; and research tends to show that it reaches people effectively. On the other hand it is a one-way medium, with the audience having no chance to talk back and to sharpen its wits on the clashing of honest opinion. It is also expensive in time and money. Good TV programing requires scripting and rehearsal and this digs into budgets; and at the same time it brings in no revenue except as colleges may attach to it some "gimmick," such as fees for registration and tuition where the course is taken for credit. Even then it proves to be no glowing success financially in most cases.

Any discussion of costs may seem out of place when one is discussing so important a topic as community-oriented adult education, but with the evening college, or the whole university for that matter, it is an extremely important consideration. It is acknowledged that television as an educational instrument cannot be ignored. It seems a practical matter, therefore, that the university take this into account in its annual budget. As a matter of fact, this is being done in communities which are in the process of establishing simon-pure educational television stations.

Adult educators are proceeding cautiously with the new medium. The following seems fairly well to summarize the thinking of evening college deans on the subject:[9]

1. All agree that it has terrific potentialities, but that it must undergo study and experimentation. Many problems are involved, and only wide experimentation will identify and reduce them.

2. The accumulation of kinescope and film recordings of successful educational programs and courses will be a tremendous aid to supplement the limited number of able TV professors on any campus. Time will not permit a delay, however, until such films are available in full supply.

3. Credit courses on TV are probably more manageable and less expensive than straight noncredit or general informational series. (Meaning, of course, that since credit is the chief motivating factor the viewer will tolerate duller programs.)

4. University information offices and the press in general

have been too extravagant in their descriptions of the early experiences of college TV courses.

It seems quite likely that the evening college dean might well consider replacing many of his formal courses offered on the campus with television programs. This plus the short course, conference, and workshop techniques may well become the most effective way of reaching the community. To actualize programs involving these two constituent elements requires a vast amount of time and a considerable budget. As a matter of fact, it seems improbable that the best job can be done without a staff charged with the responsibility of devising programs geared to specific community needs. Unquestionably, most of the evening colleges will continue to divide their attention and emphasis. Part of it will be devoted to the credit and degree programs on the campus; part of it will look outward to the community and its needs and problems. Both are necessary, but it is doubtful if accomplishments in either field will be thoroughly successful and meaningful unless each is given the undivided attention of capable personnel. It is possible for the evening college to try to be all things to all people and wind up being nothing to anyone. Perhaps Professor Blackwell has said it better. "I would urge you," he told a group of evening college people, "not to get on this community bandwagon for the ride or just as a fad."[10]

Evening college people would be the first to admit that this whole problem of their relation to the community is baffling and so multifaceted that it is difficult to know where and how they may take hold. "How do we discover community needs?" is the question on everyone's lips; and the general answer may be that we discover community needs in terms of norms. We compare what is with what ought to be. But at this point the evening college dean reaches an impasse. Where is the data upon which norms can be determined? Having determined norms, how can one determine the actual situation as it exists with reference to the norm?

The answer seems obvious. With all our sociological skills, knowledge, and techniques we should be able to make a fairly scientific study of an individual community's adult education needs. Literally tons of data have been turned up from various research projects on community life, but little of this has been applied directly to the problem of the educational needs of adults.[11] From this data, if utilized, general norms may be formulated. The situation or status of the community vis-à-vis the norms can only be obtained from a careful and time-consuming study of what actually exists. Some urban university must undertake this study in its own community, make its mistakes, develop techniques, and then make known to other communities its methods and results. The needs of each individual community will differ in detail, but the plan of approach and methods of investigation will be similar.

Such a study would be most revealing both to the university and to other groups in the community who are willing, or even anxious, to support programs aimed at curing basic ills rather than wrestling with these after they become obvious social problems. They would rather provide for adequate garbage disposal than swat individual flies. It might also reveal to the university how really infinitesimal had been its contributions to community life, not because there had been any lack of honest intentions but simply because it did not know what the basic needs were.

In all this there is much at stake. It seems clear, above all doubt, that the university can continue to ignore the community only at the peril of its own existence. There are forces at work in an industrialized, urbanized society which, if unarrested in their current trends, will either destroy a free society and thus destroy a free university or will render the university largely irrelevant. "At the mid-point of the twentieth century, America is an urban nation. It is the urban university, directly facing the problems of the city, toward which we must look for future leadership in a metropolitan society. Only as our urban universities meet their responsibilities and improve upon their opportunities can our future society be strong, independent, happy and productive of wealth and wisdom."[12]

A thorough study of the community by the evening college undoubtedly will lead to a reconsideration of its basic curriculum, for even a superficial look at existing conditions in their relation to desirable norms raises doubts about many aspects of traditional course offerings and their attendant folklore. In understanding and appraising the role of the evening college, therefore, the curricula must be dealt with.

4 The Curriculum—
Real and Imaginary

Perhaps the best way to explore the increasingly important matter of the evening college curricula is to point out what they now are, what many think they should or might be, and what problems are generated in the need areas between what is and what possibly should be.

Explaining what the degree curricula now are is a relatively simple matter. For better or worse they are day college oriented. Whether the evening college be technical, liberal arts, multidimensional, or commerce, its credit programs operate within a day college frame of reference. (This would, of course, exclude the purely noncredit type of program or college.) A comparison of catalogs is enough to demonstrate this fact beyond a doubt. Course descriptions, degree requirements, course sequences, and even course numbers are identical or almost identical in most instances. If further proof were needed, there is the testimony of fifty-five deans of the country's largest evening colleges that their offerings do not differ significantly from their counterparts in the day colleges.[1]

Whether this is good or bad may be debatable, but the reasons for the condition are hardly controversial:

1. In the great majority of cases the evening college curricula were originally constructed by day college deans and/or faculties. That is to say, the evening college was organized by the day college, and during its early years there was no significant body of thought other than that it would have a structure and functions closely resembling, if not duplicating, that of the parents. The evening college was thus in its very beginning presented by a curricular *fait accompli*.[2]

2. Even had the evening college dean and faculty had an opportunity to make their own curricula, the results probably would not have been significantly different because: (*a*) the day college curricula were convenient models and no body of experience and knowledge was available to show how, if in any way, the evening college curricula should differ, and (*b*) the evening college officials themselves were products of the day college curricula and had had little or no training or background which would have enabled them to have done differently.

3. Curriculum change has been slow or nonexistent because (*a*) it is "safer" to follow old lines, and (*b*) evening college people have not yet come to any basic rationale for modification of the old or construction of new curricula.

4. There are an undetermined number of evening college deans and faculties who very honestly feel no need for any deviation from the day college curricula. It appears that this is a minority group, but it is as positive in its feelings as the revisionists.

It may thus be seen that expedience, adherence to tradition, and lack of a basic philosophical *raison d'être* have been important reasons why the curricula have been left in status quo. Upon examination these prove to be perfectly natural and normal. As was pointed out in Chapter II, the evening college is young, and its early youth was spent trying to solve the immediate and pressing administrative problems assailing it from every side. There was little time for philosophizing. The day college curricula were old and respected. Therefore, why not cling to them until something more adequate was devised? But as time went on things did not change. The evening college dean at times found his college, even with its traditional curriculum, the target for slings and arrows from some elements in the day colleges, or if not actually attacked to be the victim of devastating academic eyebrow raising. Reservations came to be expressed or implied about evening college work. Terms such as "soft pedagogy" were bandied about. Questions were even raised in some institutions as to whether or not full credit should be given a student transferred from the evening division to some day division or to the graduate school.

The evening college dean was thus placed in the position of being intimidated by the academic tradition, and his reaction was a normal one. He damned well would show them. His credit work and degree work would be no different from theirs, and he would turn out just as good a product right down to the last semester hour. This was a safe and comfortable position for the dean, because by this means he would become known among his colleagues as a man busily engaged in raising "standards." "I am doing the same thing you are doing," the evening dean could say, "only I am doing it at night."

His refuge in this position has, at times, almost inhibited further ideas he may have had, if any, about revising the curriculum in line with the objectives of the evening college. In fact, it appears that curriculum revision became more difficult each year as the evening college accommodated itself to the comfortable dimensions of the day college pattern. The word "comfortable" is used advisedly, for no small part of a dean's reluctance to change is due to the fact that following old lines is more comfortable than striking out in new directions. No evening college dean or faculty member wants to be an academic pariah. He covets a sense of respectability, a feeling of belonging, and he finds this in his own eyes and in those of his day college friends by conforming.

What should be or might be requires more words for the telling. One might begin by reciting the conventional standards for curriculum making, such as who is to be taught, what they are to be taught, what the educational objectives are, and how the curriculum is to be organized. It seems more profitable, however, to try first to determine just what the evening college is and what its position is in higher education. Within this broad framework it may be possible to suggest some basic considerations for curriculum revisions.

What the evening college is can probably best be understood by a determination of *where* it is. That is to say, if the evening college does not yet have an identity or a "self" fairly fixed and secure, it may at least be conceptualized as being at some point in an historical process working through time. Thus, in an effort to portray what the evening college is and what its place in higher education is, four hypotheses may be considered.

The history of significant changes in higher education can be understood in part as :[3]

1. An expansion of the notion of *who* shall be educated.

2. An expansion of the notion of *what* shall be taught.
3. A tidal pull of social forces against what the university is at any given time.
4. A struggle of new educational forms to achieve an identity or concept of their own.

The history of higher education can be understood in part as an expansion of the notion of who shall be educated. The early university in Europe was a guild whose purpose was to perpetuate scholarship. The student clientele was a small part of the whole population; it was highly selected and drew exclusively upon neither the highest nor lowest families in the social scale. The emphasis was on brains. Later, the leading universities, such as Oxford and Cambridge, emphasized the education of young men from the gentry and aristocracy, which, it was taken for granted, would provide the ecclesiastical and political leadership in society. The student clientele was somewhat larger but still highly selected. In both eras the students were young. They were to play their social roles in the future, and the university experience was predicated on that basis.

We now appear to be in an era in which the university as a whole has extended beyond its earlier forms. Concern for something more than an elite of brains or an elite of breeding can be noted. The university today contains students of all ages, from all social classes, and they constitute a much larger percentage of the population than in the earlier eras. The evening college itself is evidence that the university no longer confines its attention entirely to youth. Furthermore, the university today, especially its evening and adult education divisions, is concerned not only with future leaders but also with large numbers of young adults whose activities in the market places and professions are not awaiting some post-baccalaureate date. These men and women are the clientele of the evening college; they are the voting, working, creating, and influencing components of society *now*, not of some future date.

Again, the history of higher education can be understood in part as an expansion of the notion of *what* should be taught. We are well aware that new subject areas have always had a struggle to become a respected and recognized part of the university's attention. The needs of business and industry and of political science as subject areas are excellent examples.

In the days of Adam Smith no respectable educational institution took an interest in industry or technology. Eventually the university became less and less important to its community, a situation which, of course, changed, especially in America where the university became greatly interested in industry and technology. The university as a result of its interest in mundane affairs became very important in the community life of the United States, but this condition may change again as industry, labor, and government undertake their own training and research programs. It is not inconceivable that the university may again be headed for a new period of trouble. Already physicists and chemists in our universities are deploring the fact that government and industry are absorbing for purposes of applied research countless young men and women who ought to be doing pure research in the university itself. "How can we," they ask, "compete with the salaries they pay?" Will the universities have to cast about for new purposes to fit new conditions?

In the case of political science, it came into being as a subject area field during the last quarter of the nineteenth

century. It drew for its content and personnel primarily upon
the faculties of law, history, and philosophy. It dealt with
the abstract, the historical, and the theoretical. Its emphasis
did not fall upon the affairs and problems of practical government. As a result, a group of new educational agencies
concerned with governmental affairs grew up outside of the
university. Almost instantly political science lost its theoretical aspects, and political scientists came to be interested
in training young men and women for practical participation in government. Many young Ph.D.'s went in for training in public administration, and a new tradition was born.

It appears that, in terms of the expansion of the notion
of what shall be taught, there is a kind of cycle. First, part
of the university is not meeting a need. Second, agencies
outside the university come into being to supply that need,
or university men fear they will. Third, the university, in
danger of becoming less important, tries to capture or re-
capture certain phases of the newer agencies or to forestall
their development in certain directions.

It may well be that this second proposition does more than
any of the rest to explain what the evening college really is.
The evening college does not have a subject matter content
of its own, but it is one of the agencies evolved to meet an
emerging social and educational need for subjects adapted
to students not heretofore considered a concern of the university. Instead of seeking recognition for its body of subject matter, therefore, the evening college must seek its recognition because of the *functions* it performs.

The history of higher education may also be understood
in part as the tidal pull of social forces against what the
university is at any given time. We appear to be in a period
when this tidal pull is strong. The evening college gets the

feeling of a critical period, a notion of something struggling to come of age. If these feelings have a basis in fact, it might be well to note three things: (1) A critical period or a period of intense unrest in the evening college is only a point or a stage in a process working through time—perhaps a long time. It is not surprising, therefore, that for education in general, and particularly for the evening college which is so vitally affected, ends and purposes are not clearly seen. (2) It should be noted that, although the force and energy of this movement in evening college education may be impersonal and even inevitable, its direction is not. The history of education proves that men can affect the course of that history. This being so, the evening college leaders can affect the direction of their own future. The curricula, of course, have a direct and important bearing on this direction. (3) It must be noted that although the tidal forces may be exerting an external pull, certain forces within the university are exerting an internal push. Emphasis upon certain fields, such as teacher education, commerce, chemistry, and engineering, with direct and vital community ties, represents a push which complements the pull, while certain other phases of the university may be generating forces which oppose both the push and the pull. If we understand this, it is possible to gain insight into many of the more acute problems faced by evening colleges.

Finally, a fourth proposition: The history of change in higher education can be understood in part as the struggle of new educational forms to achieve identity or a status or a concept of their own.

Today adult education appears to be an institution struggling to get a form for itself. Evening college people might derive some comfort from the fact that early in this century the American high school also experienced a new recognition of an old idea and went through a struggle to get a form for itself. Breaking from the European tradition and from the demands imposed by the universities, the American high school has finally emerged with an identity and rationale of its own.

Or we might look at law and medicine. The clear academic concepts of law and medicine are of comparatively recent origins. These two forms have general purposes. The law school may have purposes that differ from those of the medical school, but neither of them teaches engineering. If we look at how these two forms evolved the concepts of what they ought to be, we are struck by the fact that in each case a struggle had to be waged for a new and appropriate set of values, a set of terms, almost a new language, and certainly a frame of reference that permitted these new forms to be appraised in their own terms. Along with their newly won concepts, law and medicine in a very real sense also developed their own systems of rewards and punishments. Finally, it should be noted that, in both cases, legal and medical education took form around a body of subject matter content.

For the evening college to understand itself as an educational form, we cannot look to a discrete body of content to rally around. That for the evening college would assuredly be a blind alley, for content-wise the evening college cuts across subject matter lines. One major source of difficulty may be that, in trying to discover a frame of reference for itself, the evening college has been trapped by multiple day college frames of references whose concepts are anchored in bodies of discrete content. It might be asserted then that if the evening college cannot seek its identity in terms of subject matter content it must look elsewhere—to the needs of its students, to the needs of the community, and to some reconstruction of the demands which the academic tradition imposes upon it.

In approaching the matter of the curriculum, it seems well to consider three general clusters of thought on curriculum construction and evaluation which seem to have particular relevance for the evening college. Briefly, these may be classified as: (*a*) the individual centered curriculum, (*b*) the environmentally centered curriculum, and (*c*) the subject matter or essentialist curriculum.

The individual centered curriculum, of course, is organized around the experiences, interests, and needs of the individual student and has as its objective the molding or changing of individual behavior patterns. In its broadest sense it has in it much of "progressive" education at the college level in that the student's needs and interests must be identified so that they may serve as the basis of educational attention. Education is an active process, proponents of this curriculum idea contend; if learning situations are intimately connected with student interests, he will be more actively engaged in them and thus learn effectively to deal not only with the current situation but with new situations as they may arise. Hence, as Tyler has expressed it, "it is essential to see that education provides opportunities for the student to enter actively into, and to deal wholeheartedly with, the things which interest him, and in which he is deeply involved. . . ."[4] In addition to student experiences and interests, this curriculum would take into the most profound account the "needs" of the individual, a term which was dealt with in the preceding chapter and which will be touched upon again in this chapter.

The environmental centered curriculum is based on the hypothesis that because contemporary life is so complex and so fluid it is necessary to focus educational attention and effort upon the critical phases of this complex and changing life and upon those aspects that are important at the moment, so that the student's time is not dissipated in learning things which were important in the past but which are no longer considered significant in the life of the individual or his community. Moreover, it is held, the student is more likely to perceive the similarity between learning situations and life situations if the two are alike and if the student is encouraged to seek illustrations in a community of things learned in the classroom. In short, analysis of contemporary life is what makes learning experiences meaningful. The curriculum, it follows, should be organized around contemporary environmental problems.

The third approach to curriculum construction and evaluation is that the fundamental consideration should be the significant bodies of knowledge which have stood the test of time and through which the experiences of men as individuals and as social creatures are revealed. Although combinations differ they all come out as a fairly uniform pattern—the physical sciences, social sciences, the humanities, for example. The study of such bodies of knowledge, it is held, is the key to really significant and worth-while education because they deal with basic ideas which do not capriciously change. The contemporary situations to which these great ideas and principles are applied may shift with the times, but not the essence of the ideas themselves. The spirit of intolerance is the same whether it sends Socrates to his death or blasts the reputation of a modern man who because of his liberalism is crucified as a Communist. The vacillation and indecision which damned Hamlet might well be a universal bane destroying any man unable to decide upon what course he should pursue. The concert of Europe after the overthrow of Napoleon tried by every device it could invent to destroy the ideas let loose in the world by the French Revolution. The great powers failed, and the very ideas they were fighting toppled thrones and dynasties. This lesson, says the essentialist, if clearly understood by people today would be a much-needed antidote for the poisonous notion that ideas can be suppressed by force.

Confronted by these three ideas, together with the functional rather than subject matter concept of the evening college, the average evening college dean and faculty are likely to take a middle position and neither accept nor reject any one *in toto*. They undoubtedly recognize the necessity for taking into account the individual's experiences and needs; they also recognize that evening college education cannot be effective in a vacuum and that therefore the community must be involved; and above all, they would be unwilling to reject formal bodies of organized subject matter. The formula which one hears repeated most often runs something like this: The important thing is not how subject matter is organized into courses, but that subject matter be approached on an adult level in line with unique adult experiences and needs. In other words, the key to the evening college curriculum would be "adaptation"—adapting existing course offerings organized and administered for young day college students to the needs and the experiences of an older group.

As far as it goes, this formula is plausible, and certainly it represents an improvement over what now exists. Upon close inventory, however, perplexing problems arise. Does this mean that adapting the day college curriculum to the evening college is merely a matter of changing teaching techniques, or does it mean that in many instances there must be a complete reorganization of course content? If it does mean reorganization of content, should such be on the basis of an interdisciplinary synthesis or through increased breadth of existing disciplines? Should the reorganization be on an across-the-board basis or should it be selective? And finally, would such general reorganization be acceptable within the limits of the academic tradition?

There is a growing body of opinion that because of the wide range of its students' previous education, vocational experience, maturity, needs, and cultural aspirations the evening college cannot derive its self-conception or determine its purpose solely in terms of prevailing academic disciplines as they are currently practiced and administered in the day college. Strangely enough, it is a day college dean who has phrased this point of view so adequately. "I am not concerned," he writes, "with the question of whether or not we should use the lecture method, or discussion method, visual aids, recitation periods, or any other of the large range of instructional procedures in the evening division. *Entirely new courses must be introduced in the evening division,* including the replacement of some which are generally required in the day division. . . . It is also obvious that there will be the need of the substitution of different curricular materials if used in the evening . . . which will better meet the needs of adults."[5]

This approach holds, therefore, that in view of the uniqueness of the evening college's functions in the university there ought to be a bold new approach to the whole question of its subject matter organization. This new approach would not be for the purpose of achieving a complete independence from the sponsoring university, but rather toward a maturity and identity of its own, as in the case of a growing adolescent's relations with his parents. The evening college, it is urged, can justify its existence not because it represents any new and discrete body of subject matter but because it represents a new function of the university. It must, therefore, look first to the needs of the clientele it serves rather than wholly to the demands of the traditional day college.

One experiment testing the validity of certain phases of this point of view is currently being conducted in the School of General Studies, the evening division of Brooklyn College. The problem it seeks to solve can perhaps best be understood in the light of the experiences of two not completely imaginary people.

Robert Edgewood is forty-two years of age. He finished high school at the age of eighteen and went to work on the staff of a small town newspaper. He showed remarkable proficiency in reporting the news and at the age of twenty-five joined the staff of a metropolitan newspaper in a city where Spanish was the next most important language to English. He studied Spanish with the help of a tutor until he was fluent in the language, both written and spoken, and, along with these efforts, kept working away at his English prose, always trying to improve his style. At thirty he was sent by his newspaper to Buenos Aires to do a series of articles, and for the next twelve years he virtually commuted between various Latin-American countries and his home city. At forty-two he was made associate editor of his paper and settled down from his travels. Now, he decided, he ought to give some attention to furthering his formal education and enrolled as a degree candidate in the evening division of a university. He was a freshman.

Samuel Craven is twenty years of age. He finished high school at the age of eighteen and went to work as a shipping clerk in a department store. After two years of this work he decided to continue his education, and he enrolled as a degree candidate in the same evening division of the same university. He was a freshman.

Now comes the question Brooklyn College is trying to answer. So far as the technical qualifications of these two are concerned they are both equal. Both are high school graduates. Should they receive any different treatment in the matter of pursuing a liberal arts degree? Which one of these two is probably closer to the goal of a liberally educated person?

The answer is so obvious it needs no comment. Why, then, it is argued, don't we start with a goal of a liberally educated person instead of a goal of 120 semester hours pursued in a certain sequence of courses? Why don't we try to set up the qualifications and characteristics of a liberally educated person and then see to it that a student accomplishes these as far as possible, however long it takes? Thus, the Brooklyn experiment.

In essence, the purpose is to find out how mature, intellectually inquisitive adults can be helped in translating their human experiences and self-education into course credits that may be offered toward a B.A. degree.[6]

A pilot group of thirty-five students ranging in age from twenty-one to sixty-six years, and including professional people, public servants, skilled workers, businessmen, and homemakers, will have their background and experiences equated into academic nomenclature. These students were selected by a committee of five faculty members who established in operational and testable terms the academic standards for admission to and matriculation in the program. This was achieved by a series of interviews and counseling conferences with each candidate, comprehensive and diagnostic tests, and an appraisal of the student's previous record. For purposes both of diagnostic and comprehensive appraisal, the existing known testing devices for evaluating knowledge and the demonstration of intellectual ability are being used. The results of this diagnostic appraisal will serve to guide each student into a planned, tailor-made program of study. There is a combination of educational methods used in implementing each program of study, i.e., special tutorial services, independent reading and study, further subject matter testing as may be indicated by the diagnosis, and classroom attendance in those required and elective courses in which the student is deficient. At predetermined intervals after matriculation, an evaluation procedure employing comprehensive examinations in the broad subject matter fields and/or formal theses or papers that demonstrate writing skills will be employed.

In addition to demonstrating the academic soundness and financial feasibility of the plan the college hopes to find some answers to these questions:

1. What differences in method are desirable for adults who wish to achieve the existing goals of the baccalaureate degree?

2. Would such different methods result in more valuable and practical benefits to the adult than the traditional methods?

3. What are the implications of this project for degree curricula in general?

Positive conclusions regarding the experiment are not yet available, but the general consensus of those who are familiar with it is that it is working admirably in spite of unforeseen problems which were bound to arise. The dean of faculties at Brooklyn has his own explanation for its success, an explanation which has great relevance for evening colleges everywhere which may be contemplating curriculum revisions. The venture is succeeding, he states, not only because of its intrinsic merit but because *it was the result of joint planning and co-operation between the day and evening divisions.*[7]

It is perfectly apparent that this experiment, although not an entirely new one, involves changes in the traditional quantitative method of evaluating degree requirements but involves little or no change in formal courses themselves. In those fields where the student has deficiencies he will take the customary courses calculated to remove them. There are those who would go much further than this, however, and advocate an overhauling of many, if not most, of the courses themselves so as to bring them more into compatibility with adult experiences.

An example of this is an approach to the study of literature organized around certain topics or themes with which the adult is already familiar rather than around the traditional historical survey, genre, or masterpiece format.[8] Through life experiences the adult has become familiar with jealousy, the battle of the sexes, love and war, love and politics, the laws of God and man, maturation, avarice, ambition, and a host of other realities which have made up the grist of the writers of all ages regardless of the type of literary vehicle they may employ. Does it make a more meaningful course if the student can realize that many of his own experiences are the stuff out of which literature is created? Around the theme of jealousy could not the adult student more profitably study and enjoy *Othello,* "The Cask of Amontillado," and "My Last Duchess" by relating them to his own experiences or by getting around to these works in their chronological sequence? Could not Aeschylus' *Agamemnon,* Frost's "Home Burial," Dorothy Parker's "Big Blonde," and Aristophanes' *Lysistrata* be studied together as examples of writing about the battle of the sexes and thus make literature come alive for the adult? What adult at one time or another has not been tempted to sell his honor, his soul, for money or power or some other thing? Would this experience help him understand the Faustian man in literature?

If the answers to these questions are in the negative—that is to say, if the life experiences of an adult cannot be utilized in some way or other in the understanding and enjoyment of literature, then any talk about curriculum revision in literature aimed at meeting adult needs is superfluous. If, on the other hand, this life experience thesis has validity, it might well be the basis for some rather drastic shakeups in the organization of literature for teaching purposes. Literature in the abstract and separated from the realities of the life experiences of the learner may be learned, but the product is likely to be an adult superficially versed in books but empty in himself. In literature the opportunity for each individual to understand and share his own insights and experiences with the author and the group constitutes perhaps the most fertile field, not only for the understanding and appreciation of literature, but for cognitive therapy as well.

Similarly, one might consider a course in American history organized around adult experiences and problems. The adult is a participant in the life of his community in one way or another. He is acquainted with his own economic, social, and political problems. He knows from first-hand experience such matters as taxation, housing, inflation, voting on local and national issues, war and peace, crime, making a living, human relations, and numerous other factors which are a part of his daily life. All too often, however, he is unaware that these things are the elements from which history and the social studies are made. Isn't it possible to organize a survey course in American civilization around a consideration of present-day problems, along with a comparing and contrasting of these with the problems the average American has faced in his development during various stages of our history as a people? Would such a course be an improvement over the traditional chronological survey course beginning with Columbus and ending somewhere around the Harry Truman period? Would the material in such a course be likely to be better understood and assimilated because the adult has a point of reference to his own experiences? It seems self-evident that mere formal teaching of the facts of history, sociology, economics, and political science is not enough; rather the emphasis must be upon the dynamic patterns of group living which every adult is helping either to maintain or destroy. Unless subject matter is so organized that it gives the adult a penetrating understanding of his roles in society, the teaching may be in vain.

Mr. Dooley, something of an adult educator in his day, understood this. "I know histhry isn't so, Hinnissy," he wrote, "because it ain't like what I see ev'ry day on Halsted Street. If any wan comes along with a histhry iv Greece or Rome that'll show me the people fightin', gettin' drunk, makin' love, gettin' married, owin' the groceryman an' bein' without hard coal, I'll believe they was a Greece or Rome, but not before. The other kind iv histhry is a post-mortem examination. It tells ye what a country died iv. But I'd like to know what it lived iv."

These three examples—the Brooklyn experiment, the adult approach to literature, and the adult approach to history—are cited merely as illustrations of possible types of curriculum changes which might be considered by an evening college which is aware of its function in the university and which wishes to organize basic subject matter to fit the needs of its clientele. The Brooklyn experiment, as previously stated, is concerned with a different method of both quantitative and qualitative evaluation of what constitutes a liberally educated man; the approach to literature represents a broadening and adaptation within a discipline; the approach to history exemplifies an interdisciplinary synthesis of subject matter, it being obvious that if a course were taught along these lines many of the social studies would be involved—economics, political science, and sociology, certainly.

The absence of any illustrations from or references to fields other than the humanities and social studies is indicative of the fact that curriculum revision, if it is to be undertaken at all, must be on a selective rather than on an across-the-board basis, for mathematics, the physical and biological sciences, and certain other skill subjects in the field of technology and commerce present problems quite different from those of the humanities and social studies.[9] The evening college dean, for example, finds that an evaluation of the mathematics curriculum must be approached from the standpoint not only of the adult's needs but of his background and preparation for college mathematics. The college freshman is just out of high school and the presumption must be that mathematics is fairly fresh in his mind. The average adult student has been out of high school for several years and has grown rusty on his mathematics. Should these two be required, for the sake of semester hours credit, to take the same freshman math course? If not, what sort of course should be devised for adults and what should be its academic standing in the traditional hierarchy of college math courses? Must it be just another subfreshman course or is it possible to build an academically respectable introductory course in mathematics in which the really basic concepts of arithmetic, algebra, and geometry are developed? (Such a course might also be good for young day students. College teachers of mathematics say that the lack of a basic concept of arithmetic is today the greatest barrier to the student's progress.)

A number of institutions are trying out such a course, devoted not only to a study of basic arithmetic, algebraic and geometric formulae and problems, but attempting to relate these to the whole broad field of mathematics. In most instances the instructors, once they have accustomed themselves to the change from orthodox formal mathematics courses, are finding the new departure rewarding and stimulating. The student's attitude is reflected in the remarks of one adult. "This course," he said, "not only enables me to catch up on a lot of math I had forgotten but it almost makes me want to go on and major in the subject. It really gives me an insight into what math is all about." It is, of course, no "miracle course" and there are kinks to be ironed out, but it does seem to have great possibilities for solving, at least in part, the troublesome problem of the adult who wants to study mathematics but who needs reorientation. Another reason it is working in at least one institution is that the course was planned largely by the university chairman of mathematics, who was willing to take a chance with an experimental course developed with the needs and experiences of the adult as the focal point. With his co-operation the course has a much better chance of acceptance in the academic hierarchy than if it had been inaugurated solely by the evening college.

These somewhat cursory examples of approaches to a consideration of curriculum revision involve thorny problems, however. Evening college deans and faculties are only now beginning to give serious thought to the matter of curriculum evaluation and revision; thus, long and intensive study and experimentation are indicated. The problems, it may be repeated, are formidable.

The first of these is the fact that not all evening college education involves older people. There is in every evening college an appreciable number of young people (in some institutions as high as 20 percent) not long out of high school who are as lacking in maturity as their counterparts in the day colleges. If we devise a curriculum for mature adults, what will happen to these young, immature students? Or is it possible that an adult approach may be made to serve each group equally well? And, for that matter, what is an adult? If we accept as a working definition of an adult that he is an individual over eighteen years of age whose chief occupation is something other than going to college we become instantly aware that we must make elaborate qualifications, particularly when we use the term "mature." What is meant by the term "mature adult"? Is the passage of years the only maturing factor, or does maturation depend upon more meaningful experiences? What do we mean when we say that we must consider the needs and experiences of the individual? In the evening college what is an individual?

These questions take on added meaning when we consider a not unusual classroom situation in almost any evening college. Take as an illustration a class in insurance fundamentals. Let us assume that it has twenty-two members, sixteen of whom are men actually engaged in the life insurance business who are taking the course as the first step toward their Certified Life Underwriter examinations, and six who are young men only a year or two out of high school and who have had no experience in the life insurance field. Will a curriculum devised for the experienced adult in this case satisfy the needs of the youngster? Hardly. Well, then, how do evening college people go about compensating for the differences?

The problem of caring for individual differences is, of course, a perennial one in education generally and thus is not peculiar to the evening college. It is more acute here, however, than in the day colleges because they have a more homogeneous student population—chronologically, at least. As might be expected, there are differing points of view on how this heterogeneity in the evening college should be treated. There are those who urge that the young be excluded entirely; others advocate sectioning so that similar age and experience groups will be together in classes; a third group would try to make up the differences through flexible teaching methods.

While no dicta can be laid down on these three points of view, it does appear that to deny admission to the youngster may be the denial to him of his opportunity for an education. The practical aspects of this plan, too, are against denial for the reason that there is no objective way of determining when the young person passes over the boundary line between immature and mature adulthood. Similarly, sectioning as a remedy seems to be lacking in practicality. Not only would it involve enormous expense in maintaining extra small sections but it would involve two curricula, with all that this implies. There remains, then, the third position which seems most defensible. It seems quite apparent that the evening college curriculum ought to be constructed with the needs and experiences of the adult clearly in mind. Individual differences must then be solved through good teaching. In short, it is a question of whether we shall have curricula devised for the adult group which is vastly in the majority and then make adjustments for the youngster or the reverse, bearing in mind always that the needs and interests of the two groups are often not mutually exclusive.

The use of such terms as "needs," "interests," "experiences," and "mature adults," together with the questions raised above, introduces a second problem for the evening college trying to revise its curricula. Just what do we mean by these terms? What are adult interests? How, if in any way, do they differ from juvenile interests, and what significance does this have for the curricula? What are adult experiences like, and is there a common pattern of experiences upon which one can safely predicate course content? What do we mean when we say an adult is mature? He is older, but is he more mature? Is it not possible that we are assuming more than the facts justify when we say that the chief difference between the youthful and the adult student is that the latter is "more mature"? How do we get at this factor of maturity so that we may measure it? And, finally, is it not possible that this matter of adult "needs" may depend upon the answers to the other questions?

One asks these things and receives the echo of his questions as an answer, for there does not exist today a sufficiently well-organized body of data upon which reliable definitions and concepts of these terms may be founded. This is not to say, of course, that no probing has gone on. Cyril O. Houle, for example, has concerned himself with the problem of adult experiences. He has pointed out that adult experiences are distinguishable from age periods that precede it in three ways: (a) adults have had more experience, (b) they have had different kinds of experiences, and (c) their experiences are organized differently.[10]

Lawrence K. Frank feels the need for a new concept of maturity which would distinguish it from "growth" or "development." "Maturation," he writes, "merits recognition and study as implying a dynamic operation which has no terminal point or fixed norms but is continuously and progressively at work."[11] Maturity, he continues, becomes "not a fixed goal or state, but rather the successive approximations to adequacy of functioning and of conduct whereby the individual progresses from conception to death." This criterion of adequacy, he feels, is the key to a determination of maturity. "The criteria of adequacy must be established in terms of what is biologically, socially, and personally appropriate at each stage of maturation for each individual with his unique inheritance, life experiences, and personality makeup."[12] Robert J. Havighurst has taken the sociological approach and has written most meaningfully about the developmental tasks of adolescence, early adulthood, middle age, and later maturity and has established an investigative technique which the adult educator cannot ignore.[13] E. K. Strong, Jr., has investigated the matter of adult interests, pointing out, for example, that interests shift more rapidly between the ages of fifteen and twenty-five than they do after twenty-five. In short, adult interests are more stable.[14]

One might go on with a much longer listing of those who have investigated the factors of adult interests, maturity, experience, and needs—and yet the answer would be the same. There does not exist today any *organized* body of such data which the evening college dean and faculty can interpret and apply to the matter of curriculum construction or revision. Perhaps a simple illustration will make clear what the author means: A lumberman fells a tree in the forest. The log is taken to a sawmill and cut into planks. The planks find their way into a cabinetmaker's shop and are made into a cabinet for a clock. In another part of the country a metal worker turns out wheels, springs, and cogs for a clock. In still another area a chemist develops a synthetic board which the artisan shapes into a face for a clock. But all this isn't yet a clock. Someone must put the parts together into a patterned mechanism which will tell even the simplest man the time.

There is a compelling need for this sort of assembling process, not only in the field of adult education but in all higher education. For almost two generations the elementary school people have been working on a child centered curriculum. Recognizing that around the age of puberty a new set of interests, experiences and needs arise, leaders of the junior high school movement have worked diligently for a curriculum which would recognize and utilize this new set of developmental factors. The process of curriculum revision has gone on from this point with reduced effectiveness through the high school and junior college. That significant success has not been achieved in many areas is probably due more to incompetent teachers than to the faults of the curricula themselves. It is almost ironical that by the time we reach the levels of higher education we have real scholarly competence but little knowledge of or regard for the implications of the psychology of adulthood. It may well be that such a knowledge can be revealed merely by assembling and interpreting materials already in existence. On the other hand, the academic clockmaker may find certain essential parts missing, which must be supplied through new and additional research. At all events it is beginning to be obvious that higher education cannot attain its maximum effectiveness in our society unless it knows and knows well what makes the adults in our society tick, and then utilizes that knowledge in helping them to learn and thus to live more effectively and creatively in that society.

A third problem in curriculum reorganization is what has been referred to throughout this book as the academic tradition. This has been defined broadly as "a body of policies, practices, and customs which our profession has transmitted from one generation to the other."[15] This definition is more meaningful, however, if it is broken down into the specific kinds of policies, practices, and customs which have been transmitted from one generation to another. These, among other things, are concerned with: (1) a concept of what age group should receive educational priority, (2) the mechanics of the organization and administration of the curriculum— such matters as length of classes, number of class meetings per week, number of hours for graduation, class attendance, grade averages, major and minor course sequences, and a host of other related matters, (3) the organization of subject matter into structured courses, (4) a way of estimating academic standards both within the university and in inter-university student transfers, (5) a system of appointment and tenure for professors and a body of professional ethics, standards of rewards and punishments, and faculty prerogatives, and (6) a concept of the type of course which should or should not be offered at the college or university level.

It would be grossly erroneous to intimate that any one of these things within itself is harmful or unwise. All of them are part of the background of experience which university faculties have found desirable in doing their job of helping young people acquire an education. These things, then, are ✓ means to an end. The danger to educational progress comes when these become ends in themselves, when faculties take the position that whatever is is right, when experimentation and change are considered dangerous—in short, when concepts become calcified.

Many day college and university faculties are today taking a fresh look at their curricula and are re-evaluating their functions in our society, but many are dragging their feet or sitting pat with smug countenances. Deep within themselves they are suspicious of educating adults. They have become accustomed to teaching young people, with courses organized and taught in a certain way, and they are genuinely fearful that any change either in the type of person taught or in the organization of subject matter will lower standards. They are hard put to define standards, but nevertheless they think they know what the term means and thus their pain over change is as real as psychosomatic pain is to the hysterical patient. University administrative officials sometimes administer policies on interuniversity transfer students which are as reactionary as some faculty concepts. "It is a University of Wisconsin policy," the advanced standing examiner writes, "to withhold credit for evening and extension work offered by other universities except when the work is very similar to regular daytime classes, taught by the same faculty, having the same admission requirements, and with a relatively small number of special or non-matriculated students enrolled."[16]

On the other hand some evening colleges have provoked some of these fears and suspicions. They have at times not secured the best-trained part-time faculty members and have used part-time people excessively. They have in some instances made extravagant claims in their promotional materials and have thus attracted to the evening college many adults who are not educable. They have sometimes been almost hucksters in trying to be all things to all men and have offered trivial artsy-craftsy courses which could best have been given in a trade school or in some other institution in the community. They have talked aggressively about curriculum change without much more than a hunch to substantiate their claims and thus have made themselves appear vague and confused as to goals. Too often they fail to make clear to other colleges their philosophy, their plans, and their programs and then bemoan their self-inflicted isolation.

Noncredit adult courses, of course, offer the best areas for experimentation with the adult curricula. Since college credit is not involved, the tradition-minded day faculty is not greatly alarmed if wide departures are made from orthodox course concepts. If the course has a title and a description which indicates it does not offend academic dignity, then it can be developed along unorthodox lines without questioning by anyone. For this reason many evening college deans wish all their courses could be noncredit, but in considering such a step they run head-on into the brick wall of the demand of the student and of the public at large for credit and degree offerings. The beautifully engraved diploma has almost become a fetish in our society. Few people, even businessmen hiring college men and women, ever ask whether a student really has the basis for a good education or not. The questions are: Are you a college graduate? Do you have a degree? As a result vast numbers of both day and evening college students who pass through what are sometimes seriously called the halls of learning are not looking for an education. They want a piece of paper which certifies they are educated. This sort of certification, it might be said, is becoming more and more necessary for the graduate to use in proving that he has an education. Often one might never suspect it if forced to judge by his behavior, his level of conversation, or the books he reads.

The evening college dean is thus forced by circumstances to regard the external signs of the academic tradition. But this does not mean he must play the role of Prometheus. There is a growing body of evidence that the day college dean and faculty will co-operate with the evening college and help solve its curriculum problems if the matter is put on an intelligently experimental basis. In October 1954 a group of day college, liberal arts deans met at Pinebrook in the Adirondacks to discuss the role of the university in liberal education for adults. The ignorance of these men as to what the evening college really is was all too apparent, but the attitude they displayed was most commendable. This question was put to them very pointedly: "What would you do if the evening college dean in your institution came to you with a proposed liberal arts course for adults which was organized in such a way as to appear to defy all academic traditions?" The answers were of one accord. "We would," they said, "ask this dean to discuss the matter with us very carefully and thoroughly. If we both agreed the plan had merit, we would try it out on an experimental basis, perhaps as a noncredit course. If it proved itself, we would favor adopting it for the regular credit courses."

No evening college dean could ask for more than that. As a matter of fact it is quite possible that while the evening college dean is moaning about being left out of things, the day college deans may also feel they are left out of the activities of the evening college. Adult education is not something which the evening college can take over completely and then run off with into its corner of the campus. The education of adults is the business of the whole university.

Inseparable from the curriculum, of course, is the faculty which makes courses of study productive in the lives of people. As the following chapter will reveal, the problem of the evening college dean and faculty has aspects unknown to the day colleges. Because of the importance of the teacher in the educative process these aspects should be examined in some detail.

5 Dean and Faculty

G<small>ROUPS</small> in collegiate educational circles have been known now and then to toss around the question of whether the dean is an entrepreneur in the formulation of educational policies or whether he merely acts as a reflector for the thinking of the faculty. That may be an open question in the day colleges, but in the evening college it is hardly debatable. If there is to be in the university any forceful leadership in the field of evening college education, the evening college dean ordinarily must supply it or it will not be forthcoming. This is not because of any particular virtues he may possess, but because of the nature of his situation. His college is relatively new on the campus and deals with a segment of the population which has heretofore hardly been considered a major concern of the university. Moreover, his faculty is fragmented and, on the whole, day college oriented. There are always, of course, a few day college members who are deeply interested in adult education and perhaps the majority are not antagonistic to the idea, but the marshaling of sentiment and the formulation and actualization of programs and policies are largely the work of the dean. The fact that in over two thirds of the evening colleges the day de-

112

partment academic chairmen have either no or only partial responsibility for evening offerings gives emphasis to the importance of evening deans in evening courses.[1] This fact also makes it doubly interesting and important to find out what sort of persons they are.

From where do evening college deans come? What are their qualifications? And, perhaps as important, where do they go, if anywhere, from the deanship?

It is almost a paradoxical situation to realize, on the one hand, that the formulation and actualization of adult evening college educational programs depend almost wholly on the dean and then to discover, on the other hand, that he has had little or no previous training or experience in the field. Evening college deans do not come from the field of adult education, or even "education." The great majority of them come from day college teaching positions, with economics and business subjects leading the field and English running close behind. The second most important source is other administrative positions in the university, with registrar out ahead. Other previous positions include: deanship of the graduate school, of the liberal arts college, of admissions, of men; director of public relations; assistant to the president; vice-chancellor; assistant deanship of liberal arts, of engineering. Only about 15 percent of the vacant positions have been filled by assistant evening college deans.[2]

This means, of course, that the evening college dean must learn his job the hard way, through experience—and his philosophy of adult education comes in the same fashion. When we add to this the fact that annual turnover is large we come up against one of the major problems of leadership in evening college education. In 1954 some 46 percent of the evening college deans and directors had been on the job for three years or less. Even when we consider that some 18 percent of this number were entirely new evening colleges with their first deans we still are faced with the fact that there is an annual turnover of nearly a third of the deans of colleges affiliated with the Association of University Evening Colleges.[3] It is a situation in which nearly a third of the deans are constantly in the "how do we do it?" phase of their development rather than in the "why do we do it?" phase. The administrative burdens on the new dean are so heavy and varied there is no wonder that he takes little time to develop a rationale for what he is doing but rather concentrates on the day-to-day problems.

One naturally wonders why this turnover is so large. Where do evening college deans go?

The author asked seventy-five evening college deans that question, or, to be exact, he asked: "What happened to your predecessor?"[4]

Fourteen of the seventy-five were heads of newly organized evening colleges and thus had no predecessors. Information on the other sixty-one, however, is most interesting because it reveals that the universities themselves are drawing heavily on the evening colleges for leadership in other phases of university development. Approximately 44 percent of the changes resulted from the transference of evening college deans to other deanships or to presidential assistantships. When we add to this the number who went back to teaching, more than 50 percent of the changes are accounted for. The complete breakdown is as follows:

18 percent died or retired.
17 percent went back to teaching.

20 percent went to another deanship either in the same institution or in another.

24 percent went into higher administrative positions in their own institution or another. Two of these became college presidents.

The balance went into miscellaneous jobs, including civil service, business, and state departments of education. One director of a small college was fired.

If one cares for more statistical data the following might be added in discovering what sort of person he is:

All evening college deans are men.

10 percent are over sixty years of age; 39 percent are over fifty; 78 percent are over forty. The youngest was twenty-eight in 1954.

In the total group (eighty-four institutions) approximately half hold the earned doctorate; 42 percent have the Master's degree, and 8 percent have only the Bachelor's degree or less. In the liberal arts and multidimensional types the earned doctorate is most numerous.

Deans of strictly liberal arts evening colleges have been the most productive in scholarly writing. Next come the deans of multidimensional colleges and then the deans of technical colleges. Seventy percent of the strictly commerce deans have published no scholarly writing.

It is impossible statistically to convey all his characteristics, however. The good dean must be a friendly counselor, an administrator, a promoter, and something of a missionary. Because he ordinarily does not have a full faculty of his own he is deprived of faculty administrative committees and thus he is often engaged in such time-consuming routine matters as passing on the advanced standing of transfer students, making timetables and schedules, preparing bulletins and promotional materials, answering reams of correspondence, and checking student records. He works with community groups, speaks at luncheons, prepares budgets and reports, serves on university committees, and very often teaches at least one course. His is a day-and-night job, for often he is forced to schedule student conferences in the evening long after everyone else has gone home because the evening college student can come only after classes. He must be able to deal tolerantly and understandingly with day college faculty members who do not share his point of view or his enthusiasm for the evening college. He must have a deep conviction of the righteousness of his mission, but he must guard against the trauma at times associated with a feeling of insecurity or fancied lack of esteem or affection. Above all, he must have a sense of humor and the intelligent patience to wait out the transition period until his college shall have its own traditions, shall have become mature and fully accepted.

Mention above of the fact that the faculties of most evening colleges are fragmented presents a persistent problem. However, its discussion without distortion is difficult, for it could easily be made to appear to the outsider that the faculty situation is very bad. It is not, yet it is far from satisfactory. Moreover, there is a rather wide variation among institutions, ranging from fairly satisfactory conditions to those that border on the chaotic. For these reasons the author feels that although this part of the score should be played clearly and sharply it should also be played somewhat *pianissimo*.

In order to understand the faculty problem one must first consider the sources of faculty recruitment and the types of instructional staff employed. Evening college faculty members fall into one of three classifications: (1) regular full-time evening college (2) day college faculty members who teach one or more courses in the evening college (3) off-campus people in certain fields of specialization.

In a study of eighty-one evening colleges it was revealed that thirty-one of them have some full-time faculty members. However, only twelve of these report a full-time faculty of over ten members.[5] One is thus brought to the immediate conclusion that by far the great majority of evening colleges depend upon a part-time faculty recruited from the day colleges and from the community. This fact has considerable significance, for it seems that the evening college is charged with doing a first-rate academic job with a faculty whose basic interests lie elsewhere. To the person who believes that subject matter is subject matter and that teaching of one group is the same as teaching all others, this would not appear too important. To the evening college people who know there are important differences in groups and in the way subject matter is presented, however, the situation, to say the least, is hardly satisfactorily conducive to the fulfillment of the important role of the evening college in the university and in our society.

Perhaps a closer look at the difficulties will make this point clear. Let us consider first the off-campus part-time instructor.

This faculty member may often make a distinct contribution. Coming as he does from some specialized field, he may bring to the campus a wealth of practical experience and, when carefully selected and trained, usually does, particularly in the fields of business and technology. Some evening colleges have used the same people year after year and through training have eliminated many of the objectionable features of this type of teaching, but many still remain. The basic interests of this faculty member are in his own business or profession and not in his teaching. His own business or professional interests may demand so much of his time that he has little or none for work in college committees, counseling, faculty meetings, and other activities associated with professional teaching. Moreover, these same interests may make him irregular in meeting his classes. His grading at times is incredibly lenient, and thus the charge of soft pedagogy may have some foundation in his classes.

None of this, of course, is intentional malpractice. Often this faculty member shows more real interest in the development of the evening college than the day college man, and many of them teach at a considerable sacrifice of their leisure time with scant remuneration. Nevertheless, the problems remain. Their solution, in part, depends upon seeing that these people are used sparingly and only under proper supervision. The really alarming aspect of the matter is that some evening colleges, particularly in commerce, depend almost entirely upon these people. There are evening colleges in which as many as 80 percent of the courses are taught by off-campus instructors. And the reason is not at all obscure. It is financially more profitable to the university to have courses taught by part-time people. An illustration: At $14 per semester hour, a three-semester-hour course for a class of twenty-five students for the regular school year of two semesters would bring in $2100. If a part-time instructor were employed at a stipend of $700, the university would have a profit on the course of $1400. If, on the other hand, this course required one-fourth the teaching load of a $5000-a-year full-time faculty member the cost of instruction would be $1250, with a profit to the university of only $750.[6] (The assumption is that the instructor's full load is four courses.)

The part-time teacher from the day college faculty may fall into one of two categories. He may teach his course or courses in the evening college as an extra assignment over and beyond his regular teaching load and receive extra compensation, or he may teach such courses as a part of his regular teaching load without extra pay. Whichever arrangement he may have, however, presents certain difficulties.

The university faculty member, like the dean, was trained primarily for something else. He was trained for graduate and undergraduate teaching in a regular day class and academic department. As a member of the department and as a member of an organization known as a learned society, he probably sees himself first of all as a scholar-teacher rather than a teacher-scholar. As such he believes he is expected to be an authority in a specialized phase of his field. Though often exposed to a process called "general education," he still derives the greatest satisfaction from teaching advanced students who themselves plan to specialize in the same field. This motivating force flavors even the faculty member's survey courses or general education teaching. Thus, a faculty member teaching a general course in American history may race along until he comes to the period of post-Civil War Reconstruction and then spend most of the rest of the semester on this because it is his specialty.

Hence, it seems reasonable to believe that by and large the university faculty member's attitudes and practices are determined by a somewhat elaborate system of rewards and punishments. Calling these "role expectancies" appears to be an adequate way of identifying them. For example, a young instructor joins a certain faculty of the college of arts and sciences in a university. Under a system of rewards and punishments of long standing in that college he has certain expectancies. If he is a passably good teacher and shows some promise of doing research, he may reasonably expect to be promoted to the rank of assistant professor. In this position he is expected not only to do a fair job of teaching but to display ability as a researcher, possibly publishing some articles in scholarly journals or even writing a book. Having done this and served his probationary period, he probably will be promoted to an associate professorship and so on up to the rank of full professor as a reward for ripe scholarship.

For the university faculty member the things that pay off in his day class, academic departmental environment are not the things that reward him for teaching in the evening college. Some of these factors are incompatible, and these incompatibilities produce conflicts which may reduce the effectiveness of the teacher's work either in the day college or in the evening college, and all too often in the latter.

In order to test out this matter of conflicts a study has been made of the chief factors producing them.[7] As a starting point, five assumptions or hypotheses were taken. Conflicts are due, it was assumed, to these factors:

1. Scholar *versus* popularizer, or the conflict over standards. The day college instructor may feel that in the evening college he must lower his customary academic standards and merely popularize knowledge. He may also feel that the time consumed in reorganizing course material and in devising new teaching techniques for evening college work takes time that he should be spending on his own research or on his graduate courses.

2. Ivory tower *versus* community. This is the conflict that occurs when a faculty member has to play the role of a member of an academic ivory tower community as contrasted with his role of dealing with community problems that confront him when he teaches in the evening college. Another element in this conflict is the frequent ivory tower expectation that the faculty member is above attitude commitment concerning action problems, as contrasted with his inability to assume such a role when these problems actually intrude themselves into his classroom by way of his adult students.

3. Teacher status *versus* peer status. This is the conflict between the daytime teacher who may feel it necessary to retain a certain social distance between himself and his younger students and his need in the evening college to meet adult students as social peers. If, on the one hand, the evening college teacher tries to import his teacher status into the adult classroom he may find it repudiated; on the other hand, if he attempts to assume the role of one among equals it may destroy the basis for his security in dealing with individual students. Another aspect of this conflict may be the scholarly need to crack the whip and discipline his day students toward intellectual achievement, as contrasted with his need to be sensitive and sympathetic to the affective needs which he may warmly feel for the adults who are energetic and ambitious enough to take his adult course.

4. The conflict over professional advancement. This conflict may be largely an economic one. That is, salary increases, tenure, and the like may depend primarily upon his role as a scholar in the university, whereas his success in the evening college may depend primarily upon his ability to "go over" with the adult students. The natural tendency of the faculty member is to devote himself largely to the phase of

his work which brings the maximum tangible results in salary, tenure, and scholarly reputation.

5. The time factor. The time when evening college classes meet sets up certain conflicts. As one instructor expressed it to the author: "I like my evening class. It is stimulating. But the time it is offered almost destroys my pleasure in teaching it. There just isn't any good time to come back to the campus at night to teach a course."

These five assumptions were submitted to seventy-four faculty members in nine institutions having evening colleges. These faculty members were asked to discuss them and to rank them according to their opinion of the validity.

When the results were in it was found that the "ivory tower *versus* community" and the "teacher *versus* peer status" did not, in the opinion of these faculty members, have very high validity. The "scholar *versus* popularizer," "conflict over professional advancement" and the "time factor" were ranked as being very important. In addition, there emerged a new factor more in the form of a fear than a conflict. That is the fear that evening college work forces the university and the faculty member to spread work too thin, to try to accomplish everything without doing anything really well, or that the limited facilities of the university are being pushed too far.

But there are other facets of the faculty problem. Such matters as faculty attitudes toward the evening college, faculty intercommunication, faculty-administration intercommunication, and faculty-student intercommunication should be considered.

In considering faculty attitudes toward the evening college, it might be well to start with this question: To what extent do faculty members agree with one another about the

nature of the job they are doing? And quickly one must answer that faculty perceptions are complex and difficult to
characterize. However, three attitude complexes seem to
emerge: (1) evening college is the same as day college, (2)
evening college is different and better, and (3) evening college is different and worse.

The attitude that the evening college is the same as the day
college actually may be divided into two separate ones. One
group sees the task of adult education on the college level as
being identical with the day programs. It points to the over-
whelming preponderance of degree-seeking students in the
evening classes and determines the nature of the job by reference to "college level work." The other group is somewhat
ambivalent in its views. What it actually says is that the evening college is the same, but what it really means is that it
ought to be the same but really isn't. This group puts re-
gretful emphasis on what it considers the factors that keep
it from being the same—lower standards, inability of the
student to do as much library work, etc.

The group which consistently feels that though the evening college is different it is on the whole as good as or better than the day college is of supreme importance to the
whole area of college level adult education. It is from this
group in any university that the support for a really excellent program must be drawn. These faculty members say the
adult student is more mature, more serious, more highly motivated, and more stimulating. The teaching, therefore, is
more challenging in that one must go to considerable lengths
in adapting methods to adult interests. Evening college education, they point out, has less academic snobbery, is less traditional, can be more intelligently experimental, and is more
adjusted to the contemporary world. In short, this group has

discovered that evening college teaching in itself can be intellectually rewarding. No one reflects this more than the day college faculty member who is teaching an evening course for the first time and finds to his surprise that it is a fresh and memorable experience. His face may actually light up with enthusiasm as he discusses it. It is almost superfluous to add that after about two classes have been held his students discover that he likes them and likes his teaching; and they, in turn, give better responses. There is nothing which will kill an evening class quicker than the knowledge on the part of the student that the instructor doesn't like what he is doing. He doesn't have to tell them—they get it by a sort of process of osmosis.

The faculty member who dislikes his work in the evening college ordinarily is the one who feels that the evening college is different and worse. The causes for this attitude are complex and appear to be based more on subjective fixed ideas than on facts. For some there is the definite (but often unsubstantiated) feeling that evening college standards are lower. This feeling is often particularly strong in the exact sciences and in mathematics. Others feel there is a loss of prestige in evening college teaching. In some cases the deans of day colleges appear to be the chief sources of discontent by taking the position that the evening college is a sort of dumping ground for all the second-rate teachers they may wish to get off their hands for at least a part of the time. Still others simply consider evening college teaching a damned nuisance which interferes with their regular routine. But, it must be hastily added, this group is smaller than the other two discussed here and appears to be diminishing in importance in most institutions. It is not that they are becoming converts, but rather that death and retirement are bringing in fresh young people who are more acquainted with the purposes and philosophy of adult education.

With respect to faculty intercommunication, a study of nine evening colleges shows that only two have any regular and systematic formal faculty contacts for the purposes of resolving curriculum problems, discussing teaching methods, or debating evening college philosophy.[8] There is every reason to believe that this ratio of seven to two would hold true if the investigation had been extended to all the major evening colleges in the country. Day departmental faculty meetings are held and evening instructors attend, but only rarely do these meetings deal with the special problems of the evening school. A small department represented rather generously on the evening faculty may do this at times, as may other day departments which have the responsibility of assigning teaching personnel or recommending textbooks. But on the whole, faculty intercommunication on vital problems of the evening college is rare. It ought not to be, all agree—that is all except one faculty member who growled that there were too damned many meetings now. Thereby the study is validated, for one could not possibly imagine a college faculty agreeing completely on anything. Any study which reports complete agreement is automatically open to suspicion.

Faculty-administration intercommunication presents a somewhat brighter picture in spite of the fact that in the nine institutions studied none had a systematic program for in-service training of teachers, teacher evaluation, or teacher supervision. The investigators found instead of any sort of formal system "a bewildering array of informal, occasionally-used, devices which involved some administration communication, most often with individual faculty members, sometimes with subgroups of them."[9]

In the area of faculty evaluation the dean finds himself without really adequate information on the performance of his teachers. Actually this same statement could be made about day colleges in many places, but the evening college is more vulnerable because it has so many part-time people who are not professional teachers. How does a dean go about evaluating the performance of a new part-time instructor in business law, in management, or in any other field?

The only answer is that he uses a sort of "casual radar" which may be unreliable but which is all he has. This consists of "keeping an ear to the ground," listening to student comments, and making vague inquiries to department heads about how so-and-so is getting along. His chief source of information is student opinion, and sometimes this is a fairly adequate index, for evening students are much less tolerant of poor teaching than the day student. If a teacher in the evening is doing a lousy job, the dean is likely to receive a protest from the class, which in many instances is well founded, for in no college in the university is good teaching more quickly recognized and appreciated than in the evening college. The student is spending his hard-earned dollars for this instruction and he wants it to be good. Thus far, however, little progress has been made in the use of formal student evaluation of teachers, although such would be valuable, especially to the teacher himself.

In the field of in-service training, generalizations are dangerous, but it does appear that some things are being accomplished. Meager as they are they show promise, largely because many faculty members find evening college teaching different and they themselves try to discover the nature of these differences. Often a bit of pertinent information or an informal conference with them will have desirable results.

Great tact must be exercised by the evening college dean, however; the day college faculty member often resents overt supervision because he feels no need for it and because he is not accustomed to it in his day college teaching. For this reason the evening college dean often resorts to indirect methods, largely in the form of memoranda sent to all members of his faculty outlining the problems of the evening college student and of teaching him. Others concentrate their in-service programs on the off-campus part-time teacher who appears to be less sensitive about supervision. There is, thus, no common pattern. Some deans attempt little or no supervision possibly because of the difficulties involved in trying to translate their general knowledge, or lack of it, into specific situations. This sharply underscores what was said in Chapter IV about the necessity of defining broad terms, such as "needs," "experiences," "maturity," etc., and of translating them into practical situations.

In the area of faculty-student intercommunication we come to the essence of the educative processes, for it is in this area that the college fails or succeeds in its mission. It may be possible to have a very good college without much faculty inter-communication or faculty-administration intercommunication; but, if faculty-student intercommunication fails to materialize or breaks down, then the purposes for which all the time and effort are expended in evening colleges are frustrated and the educational experience largely becomes meaningless. It seems important, therefore, that this area be examined in some detail. There are really two areas which must be considered if the subject is to be treated adequately: (1) the ebb and flow of communication in a formal classroom situation, and (2) intercommunication or lack of it in situations outside the classroom. It is, of course, obvious that neither of these phases can be treated exhaustively (indeed, they have not been the subjects of exhaustive investigation), but it is possible by again resorting to the study of nine institutions to gain some insight into them.

Because the students are unable by the very nature of things to make extensive use of the library, much of the learning takes place in a formal classroom atmosphere. Therefore, one must first look here for what is good or bad, or perhaps more accurately, for what facilitates or arrests the ebb and flow of communication between teacher and learner.

Perhaps the first and most important question to ask, then, is how skillful are the teachers as seen by the students and as evaluated by administrators and fellow faculty members. The whole matter of college level teaching, of course, is involved in any attempted answer. How effective is college teaching? Do college teachers have a strict regard for the psychology of their learners? Do they attempt to understand the experiential background of the students? Do they diligently seek out new and more effective methods of instruction?

In getting into this matter the reader must again be warned of the difficulties involved. It was pointed out earlier in this chapter that the dean has no way of adequately evaluating the teaching ability of faculty members even if it were possible for him to visit all classes a time or two during the year. It was also pointed out that there is powerful resistance on the part of some faculty members to any sort of student evaluation. Reports from students, it is pointed out, are not always reliable because they may not look with favor on the instructor who needles them, disturbs them, and thus makes them work and think on their own. Often the teacher who popularizes and gives all the answers may have a better report card even though, from the standpoint of the scholar, his teaching may be superficial.

Hasty and ill-concerned conclusions, therefore, must be avoided in trying to answer the questions posed above. However, some observations seem valid.

As far as the evening college is concerned (and, one suspects, the day college as well), the average faculty member does not have a strict regard for the psychology of his adult learners nor does he take seriously into account the students' experiential background. Also, he is not likely to bother unduly about seeking out new and more effective methods of instruction. Whether there is a real ebb and flow of communication, therefore, is highly problematical. It is more likely to be a one-way flow, from teacher to student without much feedback. This is likely to be true with the day faculty member teaching at night, with the off-campus part-time instructor, and with the full-time evening instructor. Perhaps the reason is that too much reliance is placed in the efficacy of the pure lecture method.

This latter statement, however, is apt to provoke some mild controversy among academic people. The evening college student needs the lecture method, defenders of the plan say, because extensive library reading on his part is impossible and thus it is only through the lecture that he can get a comprehensive view of the subject matter. The discussion method is undesirable, they further point out, because the student ordinarily doesn't know enough about the subject to discuss it intelligently. Moreover, they hold, there is a two-way flow of communication to be found in the student's inner response, judging, and silent argument.

On the other hand, there are faculty members who will

refute this point of view and hold out for the discussion method. In view of the adult student's age and experience the discussion method is the ideal one, they feel. By way of films and other visual materials as well as books, stimulating discussions can be provoked which will tend to remove intellectual rust through the abrasive clash of opinions between students and instructor.

Upon close examination, however, it is revealed that many of the differences are semantic rather than real.[10] To put the matter bluntly, many, if not most, of the faculty members are not able to identify with a very great degree of exactness just what method they do use. Also there is no common definition of "lecture" to distinguish it from "discussion." Thus one faculty member describes his method as "discussion" and then lectures most of the hour. Another believes he lectures exclusively when as a matter of fact he is observed interrupting his remarks frequently to encourage questions from the class. To another "discussion" means quiz sessions in which the instructor fires questions at members of the class and then comments on the answers. To another it is exclusively the Socratic dialogue method.

What, then, may be said by way of conclusions regarding the adequacy of faculty-student intercommunication in a formal classroom situation?

The answers seem to be: (1) Objective and reliable data on the effectiveness of faculty-student intercommunication are not available. Therefore, conclusions are conjectural. (2) Most faculty members probably are more flexible in their teaching methods than even they realize. It appears that without much previous planning they adapt their teaching methods to the exigencies of the hours. (3) Faculty members ordinarily do not spend much time in special lesson planning for adult students. They merely transfer day college teaching to the evening. (4) From the standpoint of student satisfaction the rather left-handed observation may be made that intercommunication is not poor enough to be a major factor in his dropping out.[11] (5) No significant differences between the teaching abilities of the full-time evening college instructor and the part-time day college instructor are evident.

When one turns to the other aspect of faculty-student intercommunication, the outside-of-class contacts, one is on more solid ground and more certain of his facts. Unfortunately, however, the facts give little reason for much optimism.

If one accepts the philosophy that the teacher should know and understand his individual students the matter of student-teacher contacts outside the formal classroom strikes at the very heart of intercommunication. Through conferences the teacher gets his feedback. Here the particular problems of the student come to light, and the best possible type of counseling may take place. Mutual teacher-student adjustments may well be achieved in a face-to-face situation in the quietness of the teacher's study or office. This is the sort of thing which is so conspicuously absent in the average evening college. Nothing reveals this clearer than the study made of nine institutions with respect to this sort of student-teacher relationship.[12]

Only a small minority throughout the nine colleges felt a need for some association with students outside the classroom. Obviously, most of the faculty members were proceeding under the philosophy that individual differences in adult motivation, ability, and personality need not be taken into account, but that a general knowledge of human nature is sufficient, just as in the day colleges we find the feeling that good teaching depends not upon a knowledge of individual young people but of youth in general. The significant minority which does feel the need for individual student contacts apparently knows why and is able to give its reasons. "We ought to have more feedback from them in order to evaluate the kind of job we are doing," is one. "Personal contacts with students help develop a better spirit of learning," is another. "Unless I know individual needs and capacities, I am in the dark," is still another.

The kinds of associations outside the classroom mentioned by instructors are almost always informal. Office consultations with evening students are infrequent because of time and space limitations. Ordinarily the student attends classes until a rather late hour, or if the student is free early the instructor is busy with another class. Office spaces for evening instructors are limited. Thus the outside-of-class conference is likely to be a session over coffee or beer. There is no institutional pattern for such, however. In all instances it is on a hit-or-miss basis depending on the interests and activities of the individual instructor. And yet these informal, after-class meetings take on real significance when it is realized that a good deal of the counseling activity of the evening college appears to go on in such groups. The counseling picture, however, is rather blurred and hazy, with no real pattern. It seems difficult to get faculty, administration, and students together on a really vital plan of formal or informal counseling. In some institutions the faculty and perhaps the administration are articulate about counseling plans, but the students seem indifferent. In others the students feel the need strongly, but the faculty and/or the administration have been unable to meet the need.

Undoubtedly, the fact that there is relatively little informal student-faculty association is reflected in the difficulty which the majority of the instructors have in describing their evening students. Often faculty members are very vague and inaccurate in describing their classes, and this vagueness and inaccuracy lead to all sorts of erroneous impressions about what evening college students are like. All too often the impression is an unfavorable one when upon closer examination the instructor might have found information which would have cast new light on what appeared at first blush to be a "dumb" class. It is remarkable how the establishment of personal relationships with students may often change faculty opinions. Again it should be pointed out that the frame of reference which the instructor brings to the classroom makes all the difference in the world in his outlook. Every instructor sees in an evening class what he expects in advance to see. It is difficult to determine what proportion of faculty members are negatively minded, but it is clear that the percentage is so large in many institutions that any psychological readiness for faculty-student communication is hardly apparent.

Although, as has previously been pointed out, student dissatisfaction is not strong enough to be an important reason for dropping out of classes, it should not be thought that the negative or antagonistic instructor fails to evoke student responses. Although student reactions varied enormously within and among the institutions studied, an appreciable number of them included resentful responses to teacher attitudes. Instructors, many students say, are too sarcastic; some talk down to students; some are unfriendly. When students point out what they like about a teacher, personal feelings come prominently into play: he creates rapport, is warm, human, can be critical without hurting, treats students like human beings, appreciates evening students' interest and work. Evening students expect the teacher to "know what he is talking about" in his subject matter field, but even above this is the adult student's response to patient understanding on the part of the teacher of adult problems, interests, and aspirations.

Deans and directors, of course, are acutely aware of these problems (mentioned above), and, in seeking solutions to all or most of them, have at one time or another turned wishful thoughts to what seems to be the first and most basic step to be taken: The evening college should have a full-time faculty doing only evening college work. It is a proposition which, on the surface at least, seems eminently fair and reasonable, and it is not difficult to construct a case for it which would make it a *sine qua non*. Such a case would go something like this: If the evening college had its own full-time faculty, the interests of faculty members would not be divided and the teaching of evening college classes would not be peripheral activity. The dean would be in a better position to encourage the faculty to develop a philosophy and a course of action suitable to the peculiar needs of the evening college student. Since the faculty would find its rewards coming as a result of good teaching, it could be expected that better planning and greater effort would characterize its instructional and counseling activities. Faculty morale would improve because there would be no frustrations resulting from divided loyalties; thus the faculty could with more determination and satisfaction carry on the task of improving standards. There would also be continuity of instruction. Each individual instructor knows his job and can go on year after year experimenting and developing his courses, for he is operating within the evening college frame of reference. In short, if the evening college is expected to turn out a first-rate product, it must be permitted to recruit a first-rate faculty which is sympathetic to the ideals of university level adult education.

On closer examination, however, certain problems become apparent which somewhat dull the edge of the proposition. Perhaps the first of these is the matter of recruiting first-rate teachers for evening college work. That is to say, when the dean goes to leading universities to discuss employment with promising young doctoral candidates who are finishing their degrees or with outstanding young instructors who have already finished their degrees and are teaching, he discovers a strong prejudice against full-time assignments in the evening college. It is a problem which the evening college shares with many of the smaller colleges scattered over the country. In both instances the recruiter finds that the first-rate young college teachers prefer an appointment in a university day college where there is an opportunity for research, for teaching graduate courses, and for gaining greater prestige. They are not opposed to evening college adult education. In fact, many of them welcome a class or so in the evening and often do excellent work, but a complete diet of evening work is unpalatable not only because of the time classes are scheduled but because the teacher feels he will find his rewards and promotions in the field of research, publication, and day college teaching. The evening college still, in his mind, bears the stigma of underprivilege.

A second factor is that of isolation. That is to say, the possession of a full-time faculty by the evening college may be important in promoting an even greater degree of isolation than it now has. Some isolation is inevitable at best. Classes meet at night; thus many day college people know only by hearsay or not at all what is going on. If the evening college furthers this isolation by having a separate faculty, it stands a good chance to miss entirely what it most desires and needs, the co-operation and understanding of other colleges on the campus. Such isolation gives rise to mutual misunderstandings between those who might otherwise work together if each participated to some extent in the work of the other. In short, it appears obvious that the most successful and well-integrated evening college works closely with day college administrators and faculty members. If it does otherwise, it will forfeit much of the confidence which it ought to have. Case after case might be cited in which evening college work was impaired by hostility which grew out of the fact that the evening college attempted to do its job without the assistance of anyone else on the campus. Particularly is this true when the evening college is actually physically separated from the main campus and located in a downtown area. But it can be just as true if an ivy curtain is lowered on the main campus and the evening college seeks to function behind it.

There is, however, a middle way between the extremes of no full-time faculty at all and a complete full-time faculty. This middle way is being tried in a number of institutions with considerable success. Briefly the plan is this: In every large university there are faculty members in every department who are kindly disposed toward the evening college and find the teaching there not only satisfying but exciting. While they would not want a full-time asignment in the evening, they are quite willing to help develop the evening program. These faculty members may be utilized in a most important way. From each department the evening college dean can select one of these interested day faculty people to act as an intermediary between the day department and the evening. They often receive additional compensation for their administrative work in arranging class sections, advising the dean on courses which ought to be offered, conferring with the dean on the progress of courses, and, above all, acting as a representative of the evening college at departmental meetings of the day faculties. The total effect is to give the evening college dean a core faculty of willing and interested members. At the same time he may avoid the isolation referred to above.

In all of the above discussion of faculty members there has been little or no mention of *what* they teach in the evening college. What is taught or what ought to be taught is, of course, the essence of the whole educative process for adults, for it in a large measure determines the role of the evening college in our society. In the following chapter an approach is made to that role.

6 *A Role for The Evening College*

Tʜᴜs far, what has been written in this book relates to the evening college in the present and past tense—its development, its practices, and its problems. One ought to go further, however, and at least raise some questions about the future role of evening college education in our society. Indeed, its very existence as a socially useful institution depends on its discovering its major role, or roles, and the effective implementation of these by its leaders.

If questions about social and educational roles were concerned only with enrollment and administrative problems, it would be comparatively easy to see pretty clearly into the future. For example, it is not difficult to foresee a greatly expanded market for evening college education. Despite the solemn predictions of the demographers that we were entering a period of incipient population decline, our people continue to multiply. The stork has upset all the population charts and graphs.[1] By 1975 we shall have 132 million adults over twenty-one years of age in our population. At that time 63 million of them will be in the middle and old-age groups. At that same time there will be 13 million young men and women in what is normally thought of as the college age group, eighteen to twenty-one. Of these, some 4 million probably will be enrolled full time in our colleges and universities, leaving the educable portion of 9 million without college training unless it is attained in our evening colleges.[2]

Thus, the potential market for the programs of the evening college measured merely in terms of population is an ever expanding one. When there are added to this the growing social and economic pressures to attend college, the outlook is even more optimistic. Education begets more education.

There is reason, too, for thinking that the next few years will see a solution to many if not most of the administrative problems now looming so large in the minds and experiences of many evening college administrators. Both the evening and the day divisions are, of course, learning a great deal through pure trial and error. There is, however, encouraging evidence that many institutions are making co-operative efforts to untangle their administrative snarls. It is worth noting that, in most institutions where there exist mature programs and fairly well-defined roles and objectives, administrative problems are far less tedious than in those which have not thought out their roles, either for the whole university or its component parts.

The rate at which administrative problems will be solved will, of course, vary from institution to institution. In some cases the problems are deep and complicated; in others, barely perceptible. Troublesome as they may be, however, it should not be thought that their solution will automatically assure that the contribution of the evening college will be vital and significant. Solution of internal administrative problems may be a contributing step toward attainment of desirable goals but in no sense is it the goal. It is necessary that an engine have properly lubricated gears and bearings, but the fact that all component parts are working harmoniously does not necessarily mean that the machine is doing its work. It may be driving a huge buzzsaw tragically used merely for cutting straws.

It is not likely that the next few years will see any radical change in the external patterns of offerings in the evening college. The commerce schools will go on turning out increasing numbers of accountants, salesmen, bank clerks, and junior executives. Graduate offerings probably will increase, for there is a growing demand for work beyond the baccalaureate level; but the evening college probably will not (and should not) think of itself as contributing much in the field of pure research. The evening college is and should remain a teaching college. The numbers and variety of adult noncredit courses undoubtedly will increase if the competition from television and other forms of mass media can be met and overcome. Technical schools will continue training a few engineers, architects, and technicians. Liberal arts programs will go on giving basic work in the pre-professional and other fields customarily associated with the academic disciplines. In brief, those changes which will come about undoubtedly will be internal rather than external.

And this does not, of course, connote bad educational practice. There is nothing educationally unsound or improper in training engineers, accountants, teachers, and technicians. But for what will we be training them? To earn a better living? To get ahead? Assuredly! But is that all?

It is in trying to answer this last question that there is a tendency toward vagueness and toward generalities which are not very meaningful. Educators say they hope the student will get a great deal more out of his evening college education than the training which will help him make a better living, but are often confused, as Mannheim has expressed it, because they "do not know whether to educate for specialization, which is urgently needed in an industrialized society with a strict divison of labor, or whether [they] should cater for all-round personalities with a philosophic background."[3] The fact that we speak of "a great deal more," however, is encouraging because it indicates that in our thinking we have almost unconsciously created a dichotomic concept of roles.

One branch of this dichotomy is perhaps as follows: One set of roles is easily conceptualized. This set of roles corresponds roughly to the student's felt needs when he enrolled. It is not easy to isolate and label these accurately, but let us assume we can. We would then arrive at these obvious roles merely by repeating as a formula the basic reasons why the student enrolled: The student's needs are vocationally oriented. The student often has a feeling that he needs "culture" although he is not able to identify precisely what he means by this. Going to college may enhance the student's social prestige and position. His enrollment has a hedonistic motivation. He enjoys random intellectual experiences. Or he is gregarious and the evening college gives him a place where he can go to associate with other people.

On this basis, then, we may build this role dimension: It is the role of the evening college to provide a program which will meet the vocational, gregarious, hedonistic, social prestige, and random unspecified cultural needs of the student. The mere sound of such a formula, however, has a hollow ring. Hollow because it is so vague.

The other branch of the dichotomy is more difficult to identify and less easily conceptualized; yet it may well be the priceless ingredient which will determine not only the personal but the social effectiveness of evening college education. This has to do with the "over and above" or the "great deal more" factor mentioned above. Is there an overriding need or set of needs which the student feels vaguely or not at all? Is this need of paramount social and personal significance for him? A consideration of those two questions may give clues to the really vital role of the evening college in our contemporary society. It is a role which must be related to the social changes which have followed economic changes in this country in the past seventy-five years. At the risk of oversimplification, superficiality, and saying poorly what others have said well, one must talk about those matters in trying to discover the really vital part that the university evening college can and should play in our society.

Perhaps the most logical and systematic approach is to isolate and hold up for scrutiny two basic phases of the matter. These may be presented in the form of questions: (1) What is the clientele of the evening colleges? (2) What should the college attempt to do for this clientele so that useful social and personal ends may be accomplished?

The first of these questions is not particularly difficult to answer. The clientele of the university evening college is, by and large, the segment of our urban population usually called "the white collar class." If one used Warner's classification this would be the lower-upper, upper-middle, and lower-middle groups in our urban society, with a modicum of spilling over into the upper-lower area.[4] Translated into less precise sociological terms, the evening college serves the middle class, white collar groups, has little effect on the upper-upper group of Best People, and similarly has little effect upon labor except where the laborer feels the need of college training to help him become a white collar man.

The reasons for this state of affairs are at least partially explainable. The upper-upper man is, by and large, a college-trained person who finds little motivation, either economic or intellectual, for continuing his formal education. Moreover, there is more than a trace of snobbishness in him. The evening college, he feels deep within himself, is for the underprivileged. He still thinks of the evening college as "night school" where Hyman Kaplans learn their letters. Organized labor, perhaps with some justification, has looked upon the evening college as "management-dominated," with a "management" philosophy. At the same time many of its leaders have often insisted on a "prolabor" slant to courses in economics and related fields, and, not having found such, labor stayed away. Many evening colleges have remained aloof from the controversy by making no effort to recruit any sizable group of students from the ranks of organized labor. Too, one must consider the fact that American labor has not had the vigorous intellectual leadership which the Fabians gave to British trade-unionism.

Whatever the reasons are, the fact remains that from 75 to 85 percent of the student population of the American university evening college is from one segment of society. Since it appears quite likely that this condition will persist for the foreseeable future, the evening college must concentrate a major portion of its thought and attention on what it proposes to do, other than developing skills, with these junior executives, technicians, salesmen, teachers, journalists, clerks, accountants, civil servants, bank tellers, personnel managers, insurance adjusters, realtors, and a vast throng of lesser and greater lights which move within the orbit of the city. To be more specific, what should the evening college do for Jimmy Cavendish?

The biography of James Cavenish is like Gray's annals of the poor, short and simple, for he is a man to fortune and to fame unknown. He is an accountant in the office of a large corporation. Although he is taking courses in the local university evening college which will prepare him for the C.P.A. examination, he has not yet attained his goal and his salary is modest. He earns $4,200 per year with his firm and another $600 per year keeping a set of books during his spare time for a small grocery firm. He is a World War II veteran; he is married, with two young children, and is a member of the Young Men's Civic Association, the American Legion, and the Baptist Church.

His home life is placid to the extent of being almost boring at times. He got a G.I. loan and bought a small house in a new suburban subdivision; in thirty years he will own his home. His wife is thrifty and domestic, stretching the food dollar to the tearing point and watching the daily papers for bargains in clothes for her family and herself. She gives herself a periodic home permanent to save the price of beauty parlor treatments and washes most of the children's clothes to save on laundry bills. Sometimes she thinks she ought to have an automatic washing machine, but the television set had to come first and it may be a year or two before they get the washer. By being very careful they are able to meet the payments on the car, the television set, and the new dining room furniture, but as soon as these are out of the way they can buy the washing machine. That is, if she doesn't get pregnant again or the children don't get sick or Jimmy doesn't have to be hospitalized again with his ulcers.

Jimmy's routine is as regular as the tides. His breakfast is ready at 7:30 promptly, and he is at his desk at a quarter of nine. He takes a morning and afternoon coffee break along with the others from his office. There is small talk, mostly shop, and a risqué joke or two listened to eagerly by those at his table, including two secretaries. Otherwise, all day he juggles figures up and down and across on his lined yellow sheets and at five rushes to beat the crowd to the bus. He never succeeds, but he's always in there trying. At 5:30 he is home again. He drinks two cans of beer, eats his dinner, reads the evening paper, then watches television until ten (even to 10:30 if it's fight night), and then goes to bed. The next morning at 7:30 it all starts over again.

There are variations now and then. Two nights a week he goes to the university for his course in advanced cost accounting. Occasionally, friends from up the street will drop in, or once in a great while they will take the children to a drive-in movie. Saturdays and Sundays are spent mostly working on the grocer's books, with possibly an occasional interlude of bowling with his cronies or attending a downtown movie with his wife. There is, of course, the lawn to mow and the car to wash and a little tinkering about the house and yard to be done. And there goes his leisure time. Somehow he doesn't get around to any serious reading. There are the morning and the afternoon newspapers and the American Legion magazine, and when he finishes with them he is ready to go back to the television set. He did get into *Forever Amber* once but never had time to finish it.

Jimmy's thinking is uncritical. What he sometimes fancies as thinking is merely a review of his prejudices and the clichés which form the substance of his intellectual life. But he is pretty well confirmed in these, and is likely to conclude a discourse with the cliché that in America every man is entitled to his own opinion. But he is careful where and under what conditions he gives expression to his opinions. At the office he has seen several men ruin themselves by spouting opinions that were "radical" and out of keeping with the "policies" of the company. He will never forget the fate of one intelligent young man right in his own office who was quietly dropped by the company because he was constantly arguing that white collar workers ought to organize like labor. No, Jimmy has found that those who get ahead in his organization are those who are "safe" and "dependable," who keep their mouths shut and tend to their knitting. After all, the company makes a policy of promoting the proper sort of young men, to whom will be entrusted not only the company's future but that of the country as well. And Jimmy wants to be promoted. He wants a big desk in a carpeted private office.

Away from the office he is hardly less orthodox. He freely expresses his patriotic sentiments and feels strongly that those people who criticize "the American way of life" ought to be sent back where they came from—his views that every man is entitled to his own opinion notwithstanding. As a matter of fact his uncritical acceptance of clichés and homilies often leads him into the most glaring contradictions. He is alarmed over "socialism," but he feels very strongly that "the government" ought to do a great deal more in caring for veterans and old people. In England during the war he acquired a deep distaste for the English caste system and thanked God almost every day that America was a country where every man was equal to every other man. He, however, sees no relationship between this sentiment and the fact that, although he is not a Southerner, he believes in segregated schools. He is alarmed over growing trends toward more and more government interference in business, but he feels equally strongly that if another depression threatens, "*the* government" ought to step in and "straighten things out." This in spite of the fact that he has little confidence in the politicians who run the government. Education, he believes, is a fine thing, but it is the practical man who gets things done. Practicing hard work and thrift is the way to get ahead, but you have to know the right people. He believes in progress and new things but, at the same time, thinks that old and tried fundamentals are best and that it is a mistake to let radicals upset fundamentals. Honesty, he feels, is the best policy; but business is business, and one has to be sharp and cut corners.

But make no mistake in judging this man, for he is not without his virtues. He is a patient, hard-working, ambitious, and fundamentally intelligent young man who wants to improve his position in life. He wants more money, a better home, more conveniences in the home, a position of power and respect in the community. He wants to belong to the country club and to have a nice car for his wife, as well as one for his own use. He wants to be looked upon as a successful man who can dress well and send his children to good schools. His only trouble is that he has not realized the necessity for broadening his education if he is to have a chance to achieve those things. He thinks that merely being a good accountant is enough. He has never seriously taken into account the fact that he must in his thinking escape the narrow confines of his milieu if he himself is not forever to conform to its narrow proportions.

His little world is a microcosm, an epitome of a larger world composed of some 20 million other white collar workers like him—a world of people whose education can be ignored only at the peril of our existence as a free society. In a very real sense, these people set the tone of our urban culture. They are active citizens. They vote, serve on juries, are often elected to public office, make up the membership of PTA's and civic bodies. They virtually dominate the fraternal orders and, almost to as great an extent, church memberships. They are the people who do the leg work in Community Chest drives and other charitable endeavors. They are an enormous asset or an equally great liability, depending on what they think and believe. They may be a strong force for stability and reason, or they may join hate groups and help conduct witch hunts.

It was the accountant himself who led the way for this new class of citizens.[5] Around the turn of the century his scientific analysis began to be recognized as an indispensable tool for business planning. Around the accountant grew up a vast army of business technicians, economists, planners, efficiency experts, and personnel managers—all to a marked extent being influenced by the efficiency ideas of Frederick W. Taylor. As the tempo of production and distribution was stepped up, advertising expanded to include a national market for almost everything under the sun. Marketing as a specialty developed from its embryonic stage. The public relations counsel came into industry as the businessman became increasingly aware of public opinion in his business. Commercial banking grew by leaps and bounds, counting the money and creating the credit demanded by this new phase of our economy. Enormous new sales forces were created to dispose of the goods and a vast scheme of consumer credit was developed to make them go down easier. Out of this complex of modern business came the new white collar group, or if not "new" then by sheer size as formidable as if society had been confronted by an entirely new force.

The appearance of this "new" force marks the transition from an independent, deeply rooted, self-balancing society of merchants, small industrialists, tradesmen, skilled craftsmen, and other entrepreneurs, who with the independent farmers made up the hard core of our national life, to a society composed to a large extent of dependent, relatively propertyless men deprived largely of the capacity for independent thought and action. Moreover, they create nothing, produce nothing. They are a vast service group. Mills has characterized them rather mercilessly. "Whatever history they have had," he writes, "is a history without events; whatever future they will have will not be of their own making. If they aspire at all it is to a middle course, at a time when no middle course is available, and hence to an illusory course in an imaginary society. Internally they are split, fragmented; externally they are dependent on larger forces. . . . As a group they do not practice an independent way of life. . . . Yet, it is to this white collar world that one must look for much that is characteristic of twentieth-century existence. By their rise to commercial importance the white collar people have upset the nineteenth-century expectation that society would be divided between entrepreneurs and wage earners. By their mass way of life they have transformed the tang and feel of the American experience. . . . Far above all else they are a new cast of actors performing the major routines of twentieth-century society.[6]

In its incipient stages this new class had three choices as to the course it would follow: (1) it could join forces with organized labor, (2) it could pursue a middle course wherein it would preserve its own identity, or (3) it could merge its thinking with that of the business interests it served.

The choice was obvious as early as the Populist crusade of the late nineties when the urban middle classes lined up almost solidly with the business interests which were being lambasted by the Populists.[7] From this point on they identified themselves more and more with the philosophy of the group at the top of the power structure and in the process often became more Roman than the Romans. As a group it thought not in terms of what might be best for it, but in terms of what sort of thinking it felt would meet with approval from above. It challenged nothing. As a group it became the repository for illiberal thinking which even devout reactionaries had abandoned. Many antiquated social and economic clichés became theirs. Without question they appeared often to accept as right and proper the existing value scales and they defended ardently every phase of the status quo. Moreover, their experiences, as time went on, became such that little chance of escape was offered. Daily they were pounded by the same mass media of communication—the radio, television, and the newspaper with the best sports and comic sections. In none of these was there a chance to talk back, and none of them revealed to him the "sources of his tension and anxiety, his inarticulate resentment and half-formed hopes."[8]

Contemporaneous with this rise of the white collar man during the last quarter of the nineteenth century and the first half of the twentieth was the virtual disappearance of nineteenth-century individualism and in its place the growth of a mode of life which was urban and tended toward standardization.

Nineteenth-century life in America revolved around the farm and the village, and it was in such an environment that the pattern of individualism took form. Life for the nineteenth-century individualist was "a compound of struggle against nature and personal relationship with his family and neighbors. He met and gossiped with the latter in one of his three clubs, the church, the saloon, or the circle about the stove in the general store. Inevitably he was an individualist. His thinking was cast in the mold of the problems and relations of individuals. His social view was atomistic."[9]

A few hundred, or maybe it was only a hundred, miles away an industrial city was taking form. Into it poured immigrants from all parts of the world. Strange tongues were heard, and people huddled together seeking shelter in company houses built row upon row, all alike and in close proximity to one another. The factory chimneys belched their smoke, and little people groped through the dawn in response to the summoning whistle. On blessed Saturday nights there might be enough left of a man's wages to buy a few beers, but on Monday morning it all began again. More smokestacks popped up like mushrooms, and more whistles called more people to their jobs. Young men and women from the villages and farms flocked to these industrial cities to lose their identities in a vast impersonal system. Bigness bred more bigness. The individual enterprise became a corporation merged into a holding company. Mass production became the shibboleth and impersonality the mode. It was a transition "from an old America which assumed that social welfare was linked with small individual business and the wide diffusion of wealth to a new America that would accept great corporate business organization and large agglomerations of capital."[10] Under such an impact, nineteenth-century individualism yielded up the ghost, leaving behind only such part of its way of thinking as the business culture might see fit to use. To say that the changes were good or bad implies the existence of a moral standard where none exists. All that can be said with complete assurance is that there were significant departures from the nineteenth-century mode of American life, and that the urban man of today, by all the measures we have, has not come to terms with the city as his forebears had with the land. American civilization has become urban, but it is highly questionable whether it is urbane or not.

The new business civilization not only mass-produced goods, but there developed around it a widely accepted, almost mass-produced set of values and patterns of thinking. In its essence this value judgment system was a fortuitous mixture of social Darwinism, materialism, chauvinism, laissez-faire, vestigial segments of frontier thinking, and pragmatism. As Beard has phrased it, "its special interests were comfort, convenience, pecuniary advancement, emulatory display, salesmanship, unbroken progress in the straight utilitarian direction, and efficiency, with education as a preparation for the realization and enjoyment of such interest. Its philosophy was on the whole matter of fact and pragmatic."[11] Another historian has added that it gave a "quantitative cast" to our thinking and conditioned all America through its proliferation to "place a 'quantitative evaluation upon almost everything.' "[12] When asked what a man was worth the American all too often meant material worth, dollars. Anything other than the quantitative disturbed him, hence a distrust of theories and abstractions. He was suspicious of "culture," and, although he liked to boast of the biggest schools with the highest enrollments in the world, he often did not trust the scholar in business and politics. He was proud of his production records, his skyscrapers, his bathtubs, his telephones, his automobiles, and even his big libraries, art galleries, and symphonies. He was profoundly nationalistic, with strong moral overtones.[13] America was superior in everything, and other nations which did not wish to imitate our way of life were looked upon as being backward. America was the land of opportunity, and everyone willing to work had a chance not only to survive but to reach the top. It was in a very real sense a smug and self-righteous philosophy which encouraged conformity and was, as far as it dared go, antagonistic toward the individual or the group which challenged it.

A representative of this brand of thinking was likely to believe that the government was incapable of efficiency such as he believed existed in the business world. As a matter of fact, he felt that many of the evils of government could be cured by having practical businessmen in high political positions. He often accepted demagoguery with the expression, "Well, that's politics." He was quick to condemn a public servant for accepting a bribe but often was less anxious to censure the man who gave it. Labels and clichés loomed large in his thinking. He believed profoundly in "the American way of life" although he was hard put to define it. He resented government interference in business as a matter of principle. In practice, however, he welcomed intervention if it seemed to benefit him. Thus, the big industrialist clamored for the subsidies hidden in the protective tariff, and the small businessman welcomed price legislation in the fair trade laws. Similarly, a typical American talked of free enterprise and competition but worked diligently to assemble accumulations of productive facilities which would eliminate competition and render the position of the small businessman extremely precarious. He talked much about the virtue of savings and thrift and then encouraged almost reckless buying through advertising campaigns and easy credit plans.

He was likely to condemn labor for "getting into politics" and using the pressure of the lobby to further its ends, but somehow he failed to note that business organizations such as the National Association of Manufacturers or the United States Chamber of Commerce had long used the same methods to secure their ends. As a matter of fact, deep within himself he had not made his peace or become reconciled to organized labor.

In international affairs he was schizophrenic. He felt he ought to go along with the ideas of international good will and co-operation with other nations, but in his heart he would have preferred to pursue a policy of letting alone and being let alone. He was more than slightly impatient with countries which resisted American ideas of efficiency and was inclined to look upon them as being somewhat backward. Certainly he tended to measure their culture by their stock of gadgets or lack of them. It was difficult for him to understand how a person in Europe could be happy with only a bicycle. He evidently feels today that we ought to have received from Western Europe more gratitude than was apparent because of our loans and gifts, and is pained as well as surprised that many groups in Europe don't like America and her culture.

He was inclined to value highly the man who "goes out and wears out shoe leather" amassing enormous sales, but placed a much lower evaluation upon the creative efforts of the artist, the musician, and the writer, unless, of course, the book became a best seller, the picture brought a fabulous price, or the song was sold to Hollywood. He admired enormously everyone who succeeded whether the field was art, sports, politics, business, or even religion. When a man had made a huge fortune, he was likely to fancy himself an expert in the solution of national, social, economic, or political problems; as such an expert, he was apt to attract a sizable following.

However, he was profoundly disturbed by ideas which seemed to run counter to the pattern of thinking he endorsed or which he did not understand. So unfamiliar was he with abstract ideas that he thought ideas could be eradicated by the force of law, censorship, or physical suppression. The employer was happiest when all his employees thought as he did. He had rather be known as a conformist than a dissenter. He enjoyed reading brief articles or listening to speeches which coincided with his own ideas. If they were out of line with his ideas, he was likely to classify them as "lousy" or "radical." He was extremely sales conscious and liked to describe his method of convincing someone as "selling him on an idea."

Progress was likely to be measured in a purely physical sense. If a city had doubled its population and payrolls over a period of a few years, it likely would be classified as a progressive city. Similarly, a man was likely to measure the value of a university in terms of student enrollment or size of buildings or, above all, by the success of its football teams.

Even the symbolism changed. No longer was there much said about Jefferson and the natural rights of man or the Revolutionary War patriots who overthrew their government by force and set up a new one more to their liking and needs. Several newspapers found this out recently when they sent reporters into the streets with a document compounded of parts of the Declaration of Independence and the Bill of Rights. The great majority were unwilling to sign a statement that they believed the things on the paper tendered them, because somehow they sounded subversive. The new symbolism has become the deification of Lincoln as the symbol of triumphant nationalism and of the Supreme Court as the embodiment of conservative security, to say nothing of the white-coated scientist peering at his test tubes, out of which will come the more abundant life.[14]

It is obvious, of course, that this is not today a complete and well-rounded description of the soul of our contemporary civilization, but rather is indicative of its pathology. It is equally obvious that not all Americans subscribed to all of this and many to virtually none of it. It seems pretty clear, also, that at mid-century many leaders have modified previously held views.[15] And yet the description given above is not merely a stereotype, as anyone who belongs to a civic luncheon club can testify, for as G. K. Chesterton has remarked, "A national soul is as indefinable as a smell and as unmistakable." The seriousness of this pathology is emphasized by more than one competent critic. Their comments, on the whole, follow pretty closely the opinion expressed by Louis Booker Wright, Director of the Folger Shakespeare Library, to the effect that "although our ingenuity and our resources have given us the highest standard of living and the greatest array of physical comforts on earth, there is little evidence that these things are sufficient to preserve American society from decay. Indeed they may prove corrosive. Increasing wealth in our country has produced a sense of complacency and self sufficiency that may be disastrous to our characters and to our influence in the world."[16]

Perhaps the author may now return to the question asked pages ago. What should the evening college try to do for James Cavendish, a white collar worker with all his clichés, living in an urban community, upon whom beats steadily the fallout from his mass-produced environment? What should be the role of the evening college in his life and thus in the lives of all his kind? It is obvious that the limitations of this book will not permit a detailed answer to those questions even if the author knew all the answers. Perhaps it is possible, however, to set in the earth some signposts on the road between Parnassas and the market place.

The first of these would be one of general direction. If what has been said in this chapter has validity, then the evening colleges must re-examine their general directions and be sure their programs are such as to influence man's thinking. If what and how a man thinks is not important to him and to the society in which he lives, then our universities and colleges are perpetuating themselves through fraud, and so are our churches. Is it of profound importance that these young adults be exposed to intellectual experiences which in the long run will determine their own salvation and the nature of our urban culture? If the answer to this is in the affirmative, then the first signboard must bear the inscription: INTELLECTUAL EXPERIENCES. If an evening college does not accept the fundamental truth of this, then it makes little difference in what direction it goes.

But there are some specific items which the evening college in its role of purveyor of intellectual experiences might well consider as examples of what it ought to do. Let this be in the form of a categorical statement: The evening college should afford the individual access to and experience in those intellectual activities which will (1) give him a basis for value judgments based on qualitative thinking, (2) afford a broader base for social thinking, and (3) enable him to acquire a fund of experiences, images, ideas, and behavior patterns which in their totality help to make up the cultured individual.

Value judgments are the *avant-coureurs* of choice, and choice reveals the man. Walk into any drugstore. There near the door are revolving racks of paper-bound books. A man may choose a comic book, a detective mystery, a sexy novel, a treatise on psychoanalysis, or Plato's *Republic*. One man chooses a comic book and another Plato. At home one man reads the comics and sports sections of the newspaper and ignores most of the front page which is pregnant with vital news ·of national and international events. One man in a group situation applauds a demagogue who stultifies the American tradition of freedom. Another man considers him anathema and a threat to a free society. One man elects to support the program of UNESCO as a step in the direction of more peaceful world relations. Another denounces it as a tool of Communism. One man believes the Negro should be free to find his own place in society. Another holds that he should be segregated and confined to a secondary position. One group would see us huddled together, herdlike, in tastes and experiences that represent only the common denominator of popular acceptance. Another welcomes the tremendous flights of creative imagination of which the individual mind has shown itself capable. One man condemns all social legislation as "socialistic." Another is willing to judge the legislation on its merits and on the basis of human needs. One man holds that anyone who does not rise up and actively join the hysterical crusade against Communism is himself a suspect. Another man recognizes this as unmitigated arrogance.

And so it goes. From the selection of a book or a magazine to forming opinions on the most profound domestic and foreign policies, the individual is making value judgments on some basis or another. But on what bases are these choices made? Does education have anything to do with value judgments which lead to choices?

The latter question, is, of course, rhetorical. Certainly, education should have a most profound influence on value judgments and choices. We shall return to the matter later, but it should be said here that opinions and choices do not issue from a vacuum but from cerebration of one sort or another. A man does not arrive at an opinion without some sort of cogitation. Whether the choice he makes is wise or unwise depends upon the nature of the mental content. By such reasoning one may reach the not very startling conclusion that what goes into the mind of the evening college student is important. As a matter of fact that something important does go into the mind is the institution's basic *raison d'être*.

The words "intellectual" and "thinking" may be considered together, for they are, as far as this chapter goes, synonymous. They indicate the nature of the major field in which higher education must operate. We may again repeat a well-worn statement that the function of a college or university is to train men's minds. That it should be considered necessary to repeat this old thought is indicative of a situation in some evening colleges where this seems not to be understood. Some of them are trying to be all things to all men and as a result they wind up being only educational hucksters, crying their wares to all and sundry who will buy them, whether or not they have educational value—that is, whether or not they have such intellectual content as to influence a man's thinking.[17] In short, some evening colleges are teaching adults things that aren't worth learning, which include zither playing, baton twirling, and fly casting, and giving college credit for them.

In justice to many of these deans and directors, it must be said that such courses have been unwittingly thrust upon them by university presidents who have made it quite clear that the first responsibility of the evening college is to make money. The harassed dean or director, often in sorrow and against his better judgment, has responded by lining up a battery of nonintellectual course offerings which will bring revenue, but which in the long run cheapen the name not only of his evening college but of the entire university. In some cases, however, the dean or director does this huckstering on his own initiative, either because he has no educational objectives or because he doesn't believe in the intellectual content theory. In any case the shortsighted president and the nonintellectual dean are performing a great disservice to true education.

Perhaps the position of the university in modern life may not be entirely dissimilar to the position of the monastery in medieval life. The monks performed many very practical services. They trained farmers in better agricultural methods, improved brewing and baking, advanced the art of metal working, and performed a hundred other practical functions. But they never forgot that their first great mission was the accumulation, preservation, and transmittal of enlightenment and Christian thought.

When we speak of providing the evening college student

with a broader basis for his social thinking, we are suggesting that our times make it mandatory for the intelligent man to understand a great deal about his social milieux—and not only know about them but be able to transcend them in his thinking, particularly in any action-oriented thinking. The urban white collar mass man is often so overwhelmed by stereotyped experiences that he can neither observe objectively nor evaluate clearly much of the social pathology which so vitally concerns him. He is inclined to bear his burdens patiently and to make the best of things as they are socially. He may even rationalize his situation until he accepts or even defends his world as the best possible world, and in his smugness may challenge as subversive anything which contradicts his stereotypes. On social problems he is likely to think in terms of the status quo and ordinarily is unable or unwilling to view objectively the root of the social evil and to apply to it any really rational thinking. In short, he is singularly at the mercy of his almost impervious prejudices.

The evening college must devise ways and means of prying open the minds of all its students—if that is possible—but without fail, the mind of the superior student who displays qualities of leadership. Neither indoctrination nor propagandizing in or about social issues is tolerable. The open and learning mind brought into contact with basic fundamental truths is all that is necessary. In view of that, one of the most sobering thoughts for the evening college dean and faculty is this: If the adult student doesn't get his mind pried open in the evening college, it probably will remain tragically closed for the rest of his life.

Mills has pointed out almost dramatically this task of prying open the adult student's mind: "Knowledge and intellectual practices," he writes, "must be made directly relevant to the human need of the troubled person of the 20th century, and to the social practices of the citizen. For he must see the roots of his own biases and frustrations if he is to think clearly about anything else. And he must see the frustration of ideas, of intellect, by the present organization of society if he is to meet the tasks now confronting the intelligent citizen. . . . What the adult college ought to do for the individual is to *turn personal troubles and con-concerns into social issues and rationally open problems.*"[18]

When one comes to the matter of the individual's personal culture traits it is perfectly obvious that this, too, is closely tied in with value judgments and choices; that what an individual chooses will result in enlightenment and refinement of taste, or the reverse. Culture, of course, is made up of many separate elements. Malinowski has defined group culture as "the cumulative creation of man," a definition which might be adapted to the culture of the individual.[19] Culture in a man is totality, the sum of all his intellectual, aesthetic, and moral attributes. Its ultimate end is behavior patterns, for it is largely through a man's overt behavior patterns that he may be classified as cultured or uncultured.

It is absurd, of course, to think that the evening college can take a thirty-year-old man out of his habitual environment and in two or three sessions a week confer culture upon him as one would gild a statue. For thirty years he has been acquiring personal culture traits through absorption from his social milieu. These traits are powerful determinants difficult to overcome, if change is indicated. It is equally absurd, however, for the evening college to assume it can do nothing to guide the adult in his efforts to achieve a larger measure of cultural self-development. If an evening college dean and faculty should decide they wish to make a conscious effort in the direction of helping the student in this area of his life, it seems the effort might well begin with an inventory of the curricula—all of them—liberal arts, commerce, and all the rest. The purpose of such an inventory would be to isolate those segments which clearly have, or which may be developed to have, personal or individual cultural values, and to see to it that they receive emphasis. It is ardently hoped, however, that no institution will organize a course in how to acquire culture, for culture is not something the student puts on as a cloak.

It may be repeated that this is the most difficult area of human development which any college, day or night, faces, for the very simple reason that it has control but briefly of a limited phase of the student's life. Perhaps the problem is not wholly unrelated to that of curing mental disorders. Psychiatrists say the problem is complicated by the fact that, although a patient may appear to be cured as long as he is in the institution, he is quite likely to suffer a relapse when he returns to the environmental conditions which helped produce the malady in the first place. However, this does not relieve the psychiatrist of his responsibility to continue therapy any more than cultural relapses offer an excuse for the evening college to avoid its task.

However, individuals, important as they are, do not live isolated lives but rather as members of a group of one sort or another. These groups taken collectively make up a community. The problems of group life, or community life, therefore, must become a second major role of the evening college in our society.

There are at least four somewhat indefinitely defined points of view among adult educators on this matter of the individual and the community. One holds that it is the development of the individual as an individual which is the important mission of education. It is, this group feels, the need of the individual to know what Sir Richard Livingstone has called "the first-rate," which is really significant and from which knowledge alone will flow desirable achievements. A second group would go along with this view, but would add the factor of man as a social creature. It would place the individual and his development first but would add that the community ought to be enriched by the knowledge and skills he has acquired. The third group would somewhat reverse this order. Emphasis is upon group problems, but the worth of the individual would not be lost sight of. He would develop as an individual in a group situation. The fourth group holds that "the need for group understanding of certain basic social problems dwarfs into insignificance the need for improving an individual's cultural development or his mechanical aptitude."[20] This is the view denounced by Paul McGhee as "the cult of the Group."

Upon close examination, however, there is revealed a goodly amount of doctrinaire preachment among adherents of each of these groups and very few actual conflicts which are profoundly significant. There is no need for the evening college dean to be doctrinaire, for his institution must perform both group and individual functions and they need not be mutually exclusive. However, many evening colleges are more troubled about the extent to which they should engage in community programs, particularly social action programs. The university, they say, should not be placed in the position of an agitator for or against any particular community movement. Social action, therefore, is out as far as they are concerned.

There is much to be said for this position. There do come times, however, when a university must take a stand on community problems, when to do otherwise would constitute a surrender to forces whose ideals are destructive of civilized principles. Such social action would place the university right in the middle of controversy and that is where it should be; but the manner and extent of participation of each institution must be guided by its own ideals and policies. There is much which may be done indirectly or which is not highly controversial but which many communities desperately need. There are the undramatic but persistent problems of the urban community which one does not solve by a *coup* or by resolving violent controversy through intervention. The nature and extent of this type of community service may be indicated by a few brief statements (which because of their brevity should not be considered unimportant):

1. In many communities adult education is pointless and ineffectual because of indirection, overlapping of functions, and a general lack of purpose on the part of well-intentioned groups. Vast areas of community life receive little or no attention while others of less importance receive undue treatment. If the evening college dean knows the community as he should, he ought to be able tactfully to help co-ordinate these efforts and to give guidance and direction to group movements.

2. In these same communities or others, group leaders may be earnest but ineffectual because they lack a knowledge of group leadership techniques, community resources, and other requisites for effective group action. Some division of the urban university should provide this training, and this division inevitably is the evening college.

3. Community programs of social significance and social intelligence on the part of the people participating are inextricably bound up together. The evening college, therefore, must give all the courses it can for adults in the social studies and the humanities. Liberal education is no less a community need than an individual need. Many really worth-while group programs fail simply because the people involved have little or no background in behavioral studies and thus could never have a full grasp of what they really wanted to do.

4. The urban university is in a singularly strategic position to diagnose community ills and to help marshal the forces which may correct them. It is absurd to suppose that any given community can diagnose all its diseases. But the university is capable of such diagnosis, or it ought to be. One of the finest services an urban university can render is to point out salient weaknesses in community life and then to assist a group or groups on or off campus to initiate and maintain remedial programs.

5. The university can render another very distinct service in providing a "home" for community groups. At least one university has done this by providing a "community room" as a meeting place for all sorts of groups. There is a small auditorium with audio-visual equipment and comfortable furnishings. Adjoining are smaller rooms for conferences. The university has said to the community: "This is your home for your conferences and meetings. Use our facilities for your purposes." Needless to say, this has had a tremendous effect on university-community relations.

All these problems are not only important but urgent in time, for it is quite possible that we as a people are entering a sort of final period in our cultural development, a period which may come to be characterized by either maturity or crystallization. If it is a maturing culture, it will be characterized by growth toward completeness, by ripening, by perfection. If it merely crystallizes into something like its present form, none of the undesirable features will be eliminated. They will be frozen along with the desirable.

As we look back at our cultural history we become aware of at least two important population movements of great significance. One of these was immigration and the other was the movement to occupy our great expanses of land. One might almost think of them as a continuum: the immigrant from without who moved inward, and the native American who moved from within outward to the land. With the disappearance of the frontier and the rise of industrialism this flow was checked and turned back into a stream which flowed from the land to the city. At the same time industrialism encouraged immigration. Thus, so far as the city was concerned, both streams merged into one—from without inward—from our land *and* foreign lands to the urban centers.

Now that immigration has virtually been shut off we have only the cityward flow of our "natives" to concern us. It is interesting to note, however, that in the city the white collar son of a farmer and the white collar son of an immigrant Italian barber think very much alike, dress alike, and act alike. We face these people in our evening college classes. The names differ—Cernak, Obrinsky, Maselli, O'Bryan, Jones, Cohen, Fujihara, Morphopolous, Wong—but the behavior patterns and thinking of these do not. They have conformed to the urban pattern. It brings a sobering thought to mind. From now on American culture will feed more and more on itself and tend more and more to inbreed. The implications for the evening college are enormous.

7 *Liberal Education*

On REREADING the preceding chapter the author fears it smacks more than slightly of pontification. Such a tone, however, was not intentional. No effort was made to chart for the evening college world the specifics of how to do its job, but merely to suggest a frame of reference within which worth-while goals and roles might be developed. At any rate, since the preceding chapter has suggested *what* the nature of the evening college role might well be, it seems logical to go one step further and suggest *how* such may possibly be realized.

It is perfectly obvious that if the roles suggested are legitimate and are to be realized, the road to accomplishment is a liberal education, for it alone is concerned wholly with the mind and spirit of man. But having said this, it seems desirable to turn the statement on a spit and examine in detail some of its facets.

The author is willing to accept the phrase that seems to be in everyone's mouth that liberal education means liberating education; that the function of the liberal arts is to set man free. He is also willing to accept the thesis that "liberal education as specifically applied to the adult involves liberating him from the deadening routine of the job, from the provincialism of a locality, from the constructions of the viewpoint of narrow nationalism, from the habitual role of one phase of life to the appropriate roles of the latter, from a restricted philosophy based upon tradition to rational and appropriate adjustment within a changing world, and reorientating him to a continuing education."[1] Nor could one quarrel seriously with the view that the liberated man in modern society is one "capable of making adjustments to the changes characterizing our contemporary life"; that he is "aware of the changes taking place and understands their significance for himself and society. He is sensitive to them and has achieved an ability to analyze, synthetize, and apply them constructively in the areas of personal, social, vocational, cultural, and spiritual complements."[2] And to this may be added the even stronger statement that liberal education is the priceless ingredient in the prescription for the ills of our society. It almost staggers the imagination to conceptualize what we might be if there were added to our enormous raw manpower, our productive and distributive facilities, our physical resources, and our native intelligence, a liberally educated people.

But to be realistic one must face the fact that today the state of liberal education in the United States is not salubrious, a fact that should call forth louder lamentations than ever issued from the breast of Jeremiah. On every hand the chief purveyors of the liberal arts, deans and faculties of the day colleges, are commenting on the low estate to which liberal education has fallen even to the point of admitting that day college students, by and large, can't write clearly nor read intelligently. President A. Whitney Griswold of Yale comments on "the widespread illiteracy among college graduates" and on their "want of competence effectively to read, write and spell the English language and even more to read, spell or write any foreign language. . . . Accordingly . . . want of capacity to acquire and apply intelligence." Moreover, President Griswold states, that this is only a part of the sad picture. "I could multiply it many times," he states. As a matter of fact he feels, apparently strongly, that if the trends toward illiteracy in the day colleges are allowed to continue they might easily produce an educational collapse and cultural setback from which no university could escape.[3]

Professor John W. Dodds of Stanford is equally emphatic in his views on the state of liberal education, especially in the humanities. "Too often," he writes, "the universities have become a repository for the humanities rather than their interpreter in the broad stream of American culture. . . . Too frequently they [the professors] fail to make viable for their students the great cultural heritage of which they are the custodians. . . . Too many professors are content merely to botanize upon the grave of the humanities. Without decision themselves, they reflect endlessly, but never get beyond the stage of intellectual shadow boxing. To deal with life and yet to render it sterile is the unforgivable academic crime. Somehow the great ideas must be made to come alive for the student in his contemporary context. To that extent . . . the humanistic studies have declined and have failed to affect the stream of modern life." A recurrent nightmare for any professor, he feels, "is one in which he finds himself asking a former student what he has read since graduation."[4]

From another part of the country Professor Read Bain of Miami University (Florida) contributes the most scalding comments of all. Most of the people who are in it, he states, "are reluctant to admit that the Liberal Arts college liberates little, providing neither heat nor light nor vision; that it bores teachers and students, burdens taxpayers and parents, and gives administrators stomach ulcers." Moreover, its chief achievement in liberation is to "free most of its students during most of the four best years of their lives from working, thinking, and acting like adults." The result is that many graduates become "pseudo-intellectuals, cherishing the lifelong delusion that they are educated. . . . They leave college," he alleges, "with reinforced prejudices, smug satisfaction with the *status quo* and almost nothing of what can be called trained critical intelligence." Liberal education thus becomes "a showy failure, a promoter of snobbery, undemocracy, and social unintelligence. It is a double misnomer, being neither liberal (liberating) nor education. The illiberal Liberal Arts is a poor little lamb that has gone astray and most of its message is blah, blah, blah."[5]

"Our modern liberal education," the Reverend Theodore M. Hesburgh, President of the University of Notre Dame, has stated, "is a melange of disaggregate parts, concocted by piling course on diverse course, without internal unity of the subject-matter itself, and with even less external integration contributed by the various teachers who are prepared by highly specialized graduate schools and presently compartmentalized into the equally specialized structure of isolated academic departments. The result is comparable to a tossed salad except to fill out the analogy we would have to admit that the component parts are seasoned with Russian, Rocquefort, French, and Thousand Island dressing all at once. Clientele changed, new elements added, the substance disintegrated, teaching fragmented—these are a few of the important changes included in a realistic appraisal of this proud old badge of liberal education. . . . It would seem to follow from these facts," he continued, "that we should begin spending less time assuming and asserting the superiority of liberal education, and apply ourselves to the very difficult task of making our liberal programs in fact superior and more effective as education."[6]

Testimony such as this might be multiplied almost endlessly, not from written sources only but also from casual conversations with liberal arts faculty members. In most instances they reflect this pessimism, so much so that the evening college dean might be tempted to invite the Olympian day college critic who insists that the evening college is lowering standards to come down off his snobby horse and have a look at reality. "Standards" is a very convenient word, but when analyzed critically it often turns out to be something of a shibboleth. This ought not to be true, but unfortunately it is. Someday perhaps the day and evening people interested in making the liberal arts really meaningful will get together and co-operatively develop some real standards. As it is, there is too much pointing of accusing fingers by both groups. Actually, it begins to look as though it is no longer a question of which is doing the best job but which is doing the poorest.

There appear to be certain good reasons for the low estate of the liberal arts in the day college and these ought to be examined, for they have great relevance for the evening college liberal education program. Among these are the following, arranged in no order of importance:

1. Many students come to college woefully unprepared in such basic subjects as reading, writing, and mathematics, and also come indoctrinated with the belief that a practical education is the desideratum. These are, of course, a result

of poor training in high schools and the prevalent view of so many fathers that an education ought to be exclusively practical.

2. Many, if not most, of the university's best, wisest, and most mature scholars devote most of their time to graduate courses and research to the neglect of good undergraduate teaching. As a matter of fact, good teaching is sometimes not an indispensable factor in the university's scale of values for promoting and rewarding faculty members. This the faculty member knows. He knows that, above all, he is expected to be productive, that is to say, productive in research and writing. The result is that faculty rosters of many universities are filled with names that represent mediocre teaching talent.

3. The once existing well-rounded scholar of *universal* catholic interests and tastes, with a deep and broad culture and wisdom to accompany his learning, is now almost an anachronism. Our system of graduate training does not produce the catholic man. The farther a person goes with his education, the more his interests are narrowed. He ends up by becoming a Ph.D. in a very narrow and limited field, which process may actually unfit him for the best type of undergraduate teaching.

4. Partly as a result of the above, great bodies of knowledge are fragmented, compartmentalized, until the parts exist without any relationship to each other. Too often there exists no synthesis, no bringing together of great ideas into any sort of meaningful pattern.

5. Too often knowledge, particularly in the behavioral sciences and the humanities, is divorced from the contemporary scene, and the student sees little relevance between these bodies of knowledge and life around him.

6. It is very doubtful whether the period in a student's life between the ages of eighteen and twenty-two years is psychologically the most appropriate time for acquiring the values embodied in a liberal arts program. This is an ideal period for acquiring skills, but the immature mind can not be expected to grasp many of the profound subtleties inherent in liberal education.

If these statements are valid, and the author believes they are, they appear to hold certain implications for the program of liberal education for adults. Therefore, one may take the six points listed above and comment on each one of them in terms of the evening college.

1. Many evening college students also come to college poorly prepared in basic subject matter and oriented to a practical education. The evening college seems to have nothing unique to contribute to the solution of this problem.

2. If it is to accomplish its major purposes, the evening college must devote its major resources to teaching. There is a distinct trend in the evening college field today to expand willy-nilly into the field of graduate education. This is a mistake, for in so doing it runs the risk of weakening through proliferation its usefulness in our society. There is evidence that many of the graduate programs now being sponsored by evening colleges are substandard, but even if they were standard, they would still pose a threat to what obviously is the evening college's major task. The evening college probably should not make any serious pretensions toward pure research.

3. It was stated above that the major emphasis in the evening college should be on good instruction. This means that the absurd idea that almost anyone may teach in the evening

college must be hastily abandoned. Evening college teaching requires the best efforts of the well-rounded scholar wherever he can be found. Many mediocre day college faculty members have found to their dismay that the adult student often has an inquiring mind which challenges points of view in a way impossible for the more immature student in his day classes.

4. Educators familiar with the problem of teaching liberal arts are becoming more and more aware of the dangers inherent in the trend toward compartmentalization of subject matter. "American education is notorious for separating and classifying knowledge into special pieces of subject matter," writes President Harold Taylor of Sarah Lawrence College. "As segments have been classified and expanded they have given the appearance to the unwary of being independent parts of knowledge. . . . The total body of knowledge is not a system of classifying information but an organic system of interrelated ideas, facts, values, theories, and general information, some of it useful, some of it useless, some of it interesting, some not. The task of the college is to teach the student how to select from the enormous body of knowledge the most important things for his own life and the life of his time."[7]

It is easier, of course, to say this than it is to develop a plan for accomplishing it. Over a period of time, there goes into the human stomach a wide variety of foods. From each of these articles of food the digestive system automatically appropriates food values for the use of the body. The human brain, however, is not so automatic in its selection of values from the wide assortment of ideas which the student encounters in his studies and associations. The learning mind must be guided in ways and means of appropriating values; and it would appear that the evening college is in a very favorable position to make a distinct contribution in this area, through planning, to the end that the absorption of ideas and values will not be accidental.

There are people who fear that such planning will lead merely to indoctrination, but with adequate safeguards this danger may be eliminated. Lyman Bryson has asked: "If it is necessary for the child to have the experiences by which he will learn arranged for him, can the experiences by which the adult learns be merely accidental? The grown person will learn from whatever experiences come to him. If they are merely accidental, he will learn only what chance gives him to learn. We don't dare do that with our children. We're coming to a point at which we won't dare do that with the adult."[8] At least experimentation in the problem is indicated. The curriculum of the evening college is, or should be, more flexible and less bound by tradition than that of the day college. It is entirely possible that through co-operative planning and experimentation on the part of day and evening faculties the road from the market place to Parnassus may be more clearly marked. It should be a co-operative venture because both stand to profit enormously from it, particularly the day college. It is not beyond the realm of possibility that the evening college may point the way to a better co-ordinated and more meaningful program of liberal education in the day college.

5. Mature students in the evening college are more apt than the day students to demand that course content be related to contemporary life. They are eager for knowledge which is related to their own life experiences. It would ap-

pear, therefore, that the evening college is in a very excellent position to make a contribution to the effective teaching of the liberal arts by trying to discover how abstract ideas and life situations can be brought into juxtaposition.

6. Far-fetched as it may sound, an ideal educational situation would be one in which the student spent the customary four years in college acquiring basic skills and was given a sort of interlocutory degree which would be validated some years later, when, as an adult, he had acquired the experience and maturity which would enable him really to profit by a study of the liberal arts. "I would have every graduate of a college of liberal arts receive his degree for ten-year periods, and studiously examine their renewal," writes Walter R. Agard.[9]

Fortunately, recent experience in the educational world reduced somewhat the apparent absurdity of such an idea as this. After World War II hundreds of thousands of G.I.'s flocked into our colleges and universities, both to day and evening divisions. They had gone to war as immature youths. They returned experienced and matured men. Many of them who had been to college before their period of military service had dragged their feet and made poor records. It soon became apparent after their return to college what maturity had done for them. Education now had meaning for them, a meaning which would never have been apparent to them had they been permitted to fulfill the usual four years of youthful educational experiences. As a matter of fact, it seems that this deferred education plan may be the only way that students in some of the professional programs, notably engineering, will ever receive any appreciable training in liberal education. Leaders in the field of engineering education are concerned over the matter but are able to report little progress toward achievement of a liberalized curriculum. It is difficult, they say, to find enough time in a four-year period to get in their engineering subjects.

Between the pure liberal arts curriculum and the technical programs with little or no liberal content there exists an increasingly important zone where the vocational and the liberal are, or should be, articulated. This zone has been variously described. C. Wright Mills calls it a middle zone of a range with skills at one end and values at the other. To him it is an area of "sensibilities," constituting "at once a training in skills and an education of values."[10] Horace Kallen has called it "liberating vocationalism."[11] Dean Roscoe Pound sees it as "a balanced liberal arts-vocational education."[12] Everett Hughes characterizes it as "vocationalism with the liberal arts smuggled in."[13] The Reverend Henry J. Wertenberger, S.J., calls it "educating the whole man."[14]

The evening school of business administration (and/or the day school) seems to offer the best opportunity for achieving a genuine blending of the liberal and the professional phases of education. The word "opportunity" is used with wishful thinking implications, however, for few, if any, of the evening or day colleges of business are achieving a true synthesis. If one looks at their bulletins he might think otherwise, however. In them are recorded the degree requirements for the commerce degree. If, say, one hundred twenty semester hours are required for graduation, probably seventy to seventy-five semester hours are in vocational or semi-vocational subjects while the remaining forty-five to fifty are liberal subjects such as literature, social studies, etc. At first glance one might think from the breakdown that there is an opportunity for the commerce student to get a pretty solid foundation in liberal subjects which would tie in with his tool subjects and afford a blended result.

Unfortunately such is hardly the case, and for two main reasons. (1) Forty-five to fifty hours are not enough to lay solid foundations for a liberal education—at least as the subjects are now taught. (2) The courses represented by these hours are often taught in a vacuum.

In considering the first, one might break down the forty-five or fifty hours of liberal arts subjects and see just what the student could get. If he took the maximum concentration permitted he would possibly get four three-hour courses in English, four in the social studies, four in science, and four in mathematics. Or he might substitute a foreign language for science or philosophy for the social studies. If he took a smattering (say two three-hour courses) of a wide variety of courses he would be threatened by superficiality. In either case it is obvious that fifty hours aren't enough, a fact freely admitted by many commerce school deans.

In the second place, one encounters the fragmentation referred to earlier in this chapter. Ordinarily the liberal arts courses are taught by members of the liberal arts faculty who have only, at best, a remote idea of the implications of their particular subject for business. Concurrently, the business subjects are being offered by members of the commerce faculty who have not been trained in the liberal tradition and thus are hardly in a position to point out the social implications of their practical subjects. So both go along their merry and separate ways, with the student acquiring a neurosis or, worse, a distaste for learning. It reminds one very much of a situation which existed at Tampa as our troops were preparing to embark for Cuba and the Spanish-American War. On one track was a trainload of meat spoiling for lack of refrigeration. On the next track six feet away was a trainload of ice melting. For reasons that no one could ever discover they never got the two together.

One might accomplish this synthesis by offering a course entitled "How to Be Cultured Though a Commerce Major," but the author hardly thinks so. This blending, if it is achieved, must be a true merger effected at the teaching level. One illustration will suffice. Take the case of a course in money and banking in the commerce curriculum and a course in recent United States history in the liberal arts curriculum. These courses, in many ways, complement each other. It is impossible to teach a good course in recent United States history without discussing the social and economic significance of money and banking practices since the Civil War. At the same time, it is not possible to offer a good course in money and banking out of its historical context. But do these two instructors get together and plan a well-integrated course? Not often. Frequently the failure may be largely the fault of the liberal arts faculty member, particularly if he belongs to that phrenetically doctrinaire group which shivers at the vulgarity of vocationalism in any form, however mild.

It may well be that the cultivation of the middle area between skills and values will offer a solution of the dilemma of what sort of education we should plan for the evening college. Perhaps it should plan to offer both skills and values and see that they are well balanced, blended, and exoteric. It is possible that this will be the salvation of the liberal arts in a specialized and materialistic society. Kallen, who certainly could not be considered a vocationalist, has some rather interesting observations on this particular point. Talking to a group of evening college people, he said: "But in the whole meaning of money which is the objective that we serve in our day life; the only thing that we can do with it (unless we are misers enough to play with it and contemplate and not spend it) is to spend it. Now we can't spend by day, not until the working day becomes shorter. Our spending is all by night, and so our lives are divided into day life and a night life; and vocational education, as it is called, is focused on the day life which is the business of earning a living. But the rest of education is focused or is directed toward— it has no focus as yet—the night life in which men live their lives, for it is by night when you finish the day's work and change and wash up that you can eat like a human being and enjoy the diversities of the arts and sciences and beauty that make the substance of living. . . . I can't conceive that this antithesis between vocation and culture, between day life and night life is a necessary or an inevitable one. I think that the chief function of the evening college on which the survival and growth, it seems to me, in the long run is pretty sure to depend, is to *work out the methods by which that antithesis is to become an orchestration,* for to begin with, one man's vocation provides the substance of another man's culture."[15]

When the world of business and industry is surveyed, what is apparently a paradoxical situation is discovered. In the words of one prominent business leader: "Every year more and more business men talk about the importance of liberal arts education. Yet when the managers of their employment offices go around to colleges they take up about one liberal arts graduate for a hundred engineers or graduates of some other specialized training."[16] "Our business systems," another writes, "indeed, our whole scheme of contemporary American life, requires the education of men and women of moral stamina who can think and who can *discriminate among values.* This implies the necessity for the *continued extension of a sound liberal education* for every American boy and girl with the capacity to assimilate it."[17] But in 1952 when business went on its annual trek to the colleges in search of talent, only sixteen out of one hundred seventeen manufacturing concerns were willing to consider the liberal arts graduate. In 1954 the first two hundred recruiters who came to the campus of a large university expressed their preferences as follows: one hundred forty-five engineers, thirty-nine other specialists, sixteen liberal arts majors.[18]

Outside the fields of engineering and science it appears that what business and industry want for most jobs is men with a liberal education in values but who also have a basic orientation toward skills. In fact, one leader says this in so many words. "The truth of the matter is," he says, "that we need both broadly educated people and specialized education, preferably incorporated in the same B.A. degree."[19] It would appear that it is this basic orientation toward skills and not specific skills themselves which business wants. "Once we have employed a college graduate," another business leader writes, "a tailor-made training program is mapped out for him. . . . Training is primarily the job of business, and education is the job of the schools."[20] In short, business can supply the deficiency in skills and not the deficiency in education.

Neither the world of business nor society in general, however, is one whit concerned over the question of whether a man gets his education in the day time or in the evening, or at what age he gets it. Evening colleges and day colleges must, therefore, join hands in the process of education, for they are but artificial administrative divisions of a movement which has so much to do with the shaping of our national destiny. Higher education must by its very nature play a large part in answering a series of pungent questions propounded by Henry Steele Commager:

Out of their environment and experience Americans have fashioned a distinctive character. Can we preserve and develop the best in that character in a changed environment and under the impact of a new set of historical experiences?

We have been wonderfully inventive in the physical and technological realm. Can we prove equally resourceful in the realms of social institutions and of morals?

We have achieved the highest standard of living ever known to man. How will we live?

Our society has changed from rural to urban. Will we learn to master the city as our fathers did the land?

We have created an economy of abundance. Can we fashion a political mechanism to assure the equitable distribution of that abundance?

We are democratic in law. Will we be democratic in fact?

Our culture has been derivative. Can we create a culture of our own?

We have the largest educational system in the world. For what will we educate?

We have questioned the validity of old moral codes. Can we formulate new ones as effective?

We are pragmatic. Can we preserve our pragmatism from vulgarization?

We are intelligent. Will that intelligence be applied to the solution of our problems?[21]

NOTES, BIBLIOGRAPHY, AND INDEX

Notes

NOTES TO CHAPTER I

[1] In the great majority of cases the evening college is located on the main campus. In a few instances the evening college has a separate downtown unit.

[2] Paul McGhee, *A School for Optimists* ("Notes and Essays on Education for Adults," No. 6, August 1953 [Chicago: The Center for the Study of Liberal Education for Adults]), 2-3.

[3] All cases cited are real, not imaginary.

[4] By adult in our context is meant any person over eighteen years of age who is taking work in college but whose chief interests and activities are outside the field of the classroom. The term "adult education" as used here means a program in which adults are enrolled for formal training in a more or less systematic manner.

[5] From an unpublished study by the staff of the Center for the Study of Liberal Education for Adults. See also James T. Carey, *Why Students Drop Out: A Study of Evening College Student Motivation* (Chicago: The Center for the Study of Liberal Education for Adults, 1953).

[6] Peter E. Siegle, "Mountains, Plateaus, and Valleys in Adult Learning," *Adult Education*, IV, No. 4 (March 1954), 146.

[7] Frank S. Freeman, *Individual Differences* (New York, 1934), 287.

[8] Sidney L. Pressey, J. Elliot Janney, and Raymond G. Kuhlen, *Life: A Psychological Survey* (New York, 1939).

[9] As reported in the *New Orleans Times-Picayune*, February 8, 1954.

[10] As reported by John B. Schwertman, Director of the Center for the Study of Liberal Education for Adults.

[11] See Raymond G. Kuhlen and others, *The Psychology of Human Development* (New York, 1949).

BF
131->ol
P>

[12] See Pressey, Janney, and Kuhlen, *Life: A Psychological Survey*, 220 ff.

[13] Cf. Carey, *Why Students Drop Out*, 18.

[14] This would tend to confirm the observation that adults fear course grades, while at the same time they want to be evaluated. That is, although they put demands on the instructor to let them know "How am I doing?" they resent being compared with their fellow students.

[15] Siegle, "Mountains, Plateaus, and Valleys in Adult Learning," 150.

NOTES TO CHAPTER II

[1] This classification is made from the membership roster of the Association of University Evening Colleges as it existed in 1953.

[2] An interesting summary of this period of American education is found in Merle Curti, *The Growth of American Thought* (New York, 1943), Chap. XXIII.

[3] *Ibid.*, 593.

[4] W. S. Bittner, *The University Extension Movement*, Bulletin 1919, No. 84, Bureau of Education (Washington, D.C.: Government Printing Office, 1920), 14.

[5] Cyril O. Houle, *University Adult Education in the United States* (undated pamphlet).

[6] *Ibid.* Herbert Baxter Adams in 1900 listed the deficiencies of the extension movement as: (1) lack of suitable extension lecturers; (2) lack of financial support; (3) the vast distances to be traversed by university men already overworked; (4) the necessity and greater importance of academic service on college and university premises; and (5) the recognition of better and less expensive instrumentalities for popular education. *Report of the Commissioner of Education for the Year 1899-1900* (Washington, D.C.: Government Printing Office, 1901) I, 305. Donald Slesinger and Elizabeth Mead in *Encyclopedia of the Social Sciences*, VIII, 187, state flatly that the decline was due largely to the fact that "they did not adapt their courses to the needs of the new audiences." John R. Morton, *University Extension in the United States* (University of Alabama

Press, 1953) does not discuss this phase of the extension movement.

[7] R. H. Eckelberry, *The History of the Municipal University in the United States*, Bulletin 1932, No. 2, Office of Education (Washington, D.C.: Government Printing Office), 7.

[8] *Ibid.*, 187, 190.

[9] James Bryce, *The American Commonwealth* (2 vols.; New York, 1888), II, 2.

[10] A survey of the fifty-five largest evening colleges shows that in thirty-two cases the action setting up the evening college was that of the president. This survey will be cited hereafter as "Survey of Fifty-five Evening Colleges."

[11] The urban nature of the evening college may be determined from the fact that of the fifty-five largest, only one is located in a city under 100,000 population. *Ibid.*

[12] The pressure of public demand and demands of business groups were responsible for the organization of forty-seven of the fifty-five largest evening colleges. The other twelve appear to have been solely on the initiative of the universities themselves. *Ibid.*

[13] Of the fifty-five evening colleges studied only fourteen are located in public tax-supported institutions. *Ibid.*

[14] *Proceedings of the Twentieth Annual Meeting of the Association of Urban Universities* (1933), Introduction.

[15] This account is based on information supplied the author by Robert A. Love of City College, New York, David Henry, President of the University of Illinois, and Henry C. Mills of the University of Rochester, who were present at the meeting.

[16] John Waters to Cyril O. Houle, October 25, 1953. This is one of a series of letters to Mr. Houle from deans and directors on the subject of evening college problems and goals. Referred to hereafter as "Houle file."

[17] This information was obtained from Frank R. Neuffer, *Administrative Policies and Practices of Evening Colleges* (Chicago: The Center for the Study of Liberal Education for Adults, 1953).

[18] Fifth Interim Report of John B. Schwertman, Director of the Center, January 15, 1954.

[19] Paul McGhee, "Three Dimensions of Adult Education," an address delivered at the thirty-sixth annual meeting of the American Council on Education, October 9, 1953.

20 In *Proceedings of the Association of University Evening Colleges, 1953* (Fifteenth Annual Meeting), 55.

NOTES TO CHAPTER III

1 In *Proceedings of the Association of University Evening Colleges, 1953*, 28-31.

2 An interesting and valuable treatment of this subject is in Floyd Hunter, *Community Power Structure* (Chapel Hill, 1953).

3 Robert J. Havighurst, *Social Roles of the Middle-Aged Person* ("Notes and Essays on Education for Adults," No 4 [Chicago: The Center for the Study of Liberal Education for Adults, 1953]).

4 Ralph W. Tyler, *Basic Principles of Curriculum and Instruction* (Chicago, 1950), 6.

5 See C. Wright Mills, *Mass Society and Liberal Education* ("Notes and Essays on Education for Adults," No. 9 [Chicago: The Center for the Study of Liberal Education for Adults, 1954]).

6 *Patterns of Liberal Education in the Evening College: A Case Study of Nine Institutions* (Chicago: The Center for the Study of Liberal Education for Adults, 1952), 9-10.

7 These excerpts are from letters written to Cyril O. Houle as program material for the 1953 meeting of the Association of University Evening Colleges. Cited hereafter as "Houle correspondence." Because the writers of these letters did not expect them to be published, anonymity is preserved.

8 Ralph B. Spence and Max Wolff, "Adult Education and Community Development," *Review of Educational Research*, XXIII, No. 3 (June 1953), 254.

9 *Proceedings of the Association of University Evening Colleges, 1953*, 62. See also *Television and the University* (Chicago: The Center for the Study of Liberal Education for Adults, 1953).

10 *Ibid.*, 33.

11 Preliminary studies have been made in several urban areas. For a listing of these, see *Review of Educational Research*, XXIII, No. 3 (June 1953), 256-260

12 President John Schoff Millis of Western Reserve University in Association of Urban Universities *Newsletter*, February 15, 1952.

NOTES TO CHAPTER IV

[1] "Survey of Fifty-five Evening Colleges." Only ten deans report any significant differences, and five of them have noncredit-type institutions.

[2] *Ibid.* The curricula of only twelve evening colleges were set up largely by the evening college dean and faculty.

[3] From the original draft of a document prepared by John Schwertman and the staff of the Center for the Study of Liberal Education for Adults for a workshop of evening college deans, September 1953.

[4] Ralph W. Tyler, *Basic Principles of Curriculum and Instruction* (Chicago, 1950), 8.

[5] Ralph F. Strebel, Dean of Utica College of Syracuse University, to the author.

[6] A summary of the experiment was furnished the author by Edwin H. Spengler, Director of the School of General Studies.

[7] Dean William R. Gaede to the author.

[8] See Russell F. W. Smith, *Themes and Variations: An Invitation to Literature* (Chicago: The Center for the Study of Liberal Education for Adults, 1953).

[9] This is not intended to say that mathematics and science do not contain values as well as skills.

[10] Quoted by John Schwertman in a paper entitled "Explicitly for Adults," presented at the 1954 annual meeting of the Association of University Evening Colleges, Milwaukee, Wisconsin. Mr. Schwertman is quoting from one of Professor Houle's lectures.

[11] Lawrence W. Frank, "The Concept of Maturity," *Child Development*, XXI (March 1950), 23.

[12] Lawrence W. Frank, "Gerontology," *Journal of Gerontology*, I (January 1946), 5-6.

[13] Lawrence W. Frank, *Human Development and Education* (New York, 1953).

[14] Edward K. Strong, *Change of Interest with Age* (Stanford University Press, 1931).

[15] Earl McGrath in *Proceedings of the Association of University Evening Colleges, 1953*, 21.

[16] Florence C. Challoner to Florence W. Toppino, Registrar of Tulane University, May 11, 1954.

NOTES TO CHAPTER V

[1] Neuffer, *Administrative Policies and Practices of Evening Colleges*, 3.

[2] These data were taken from the official directory of the Association of University Evening Colleges, 1954, compiled and edited by Bernard Reed of the University of Cincinnati.

[3] *Ibid.*

[4] Via a questionnaire, of course.

[5] Neuffer, *Administrative Policies and Practices of Evening Colleges*, 6.

[6] The word "profit" is used cautiously. There are, of course, costs other than instruction, such as overhead, depreciation, etc.

[7] The study was conducted by John Schwertman, Director of the Center for the Study of Liberal Education for Adults, during 1955. It is as yet unpublished.

[8] The author has borrowed heavily from a pioneering piece of research entitled *Patterns of Liberal Education in the Evening College: A Case Study of Nine Institutions* (1952), developed and published by the Center for the Study of Liberal Education for Adults. The nine institutions were: Akron, Chicago, Cincinnati, Detroit, Louisville, New York, Northwestern, Southern California, and Western Reserve.

[9] *Ibid.*, 19.

[10] *Ibid.*, 52.

[11] Carey, *Why Students Drop Out*, 29-32.

[12] *Patterns of Liberal Education in the Evening College*, 22-23.

NOTES TO CHAPTER VI

[1] See David Riesman, *The Lonely Crowd: A Study of the Changing American Character* (New Haven, 1950), Chapter I. See also Dennis H. Wrong, "The Stork Surprises the Demographers," *Commentary*, October 1952, 375-382.

[2] Ronald B. Thompson and Thomas Crane in *The Impending*

Tidal Wave of Students (Bulletin of the American Association of Collegiate Registrars and Admissions Officers, October 1954), 22, estimates an enrollment of slightly over 4 million in 1970-1971, provided approximately one third of the eligible youth attend college.

³ Karl Mannheim, *Diagnosis of Our Times* (New York, 1944), 16.

⁴ See W. Lloyd Warner and Paul S. Lunt, *The Social Life of a Modern Community* (4 vols.; New Haven, 1941), I, 332. For purposes of sociological investigation the community is divided into classes as follows: Upper-upper; lower-upper; upper-middle; lower-middle; upper-lower; lower-lower.

⁵ Harvey Wish, *Contemporary America* (New York, 1948), 5.

⁶ C. Wright Mills, *White Collar: The American Middle Classes* (New York, 1951), IX.

⁷ Eric Goldman, *Rendezvous with Destiny* (New York, 1953), 60-61.

⁸ C. Wright Mills, *Mass Society and Liberal Education* ("Notes and Essays on Education for Adults," No. 9 [Chicago: The Center for the Study of Liberal Education for Adults, 1954]), 13.

⁹ Ralph H. Gabriel, *The Course of American Democratic Thought* (New York, 1940), 7-8.

¹⁰ Louis M. Hacker and Helene S. Zahler, *The United States in the 20th Century* (New York, 1952), 3-4.

¹¹ Charles A. and Mary E. Beard, *America in Midpassage* (New York, 1939), 862.

¹² Henry Steele Commager, *The American Mind* (Yale University Press, 1952), 7.

¹³ *Ibid.*, 8-18.

¹⁴ Gabriel, *The Course of American Democratic Thought*, 9-19.

¹⁵ For the virtues of the new business leader and his philosophy, see Frederick L. Allen, *The Big Change* (New York, 1952); *U.S.A., The Permanent Revolution* by the editors of *Fortune* (New York, 1951).

¹⁶ John Schwertman, Director of the Center for the Study of Liberal Education for Adults, suggested to a faculty seminar on adult education at Springfield, Massachusetts, criteria which could be used to help a university accept or reject certain educational activities. These were: 1. To what extent is the subject matter

complex? 2. Is there a primary concern for intellectual development? 3. To what extent will an educational activity tend to enlarge social and/or esthetic experience? 4. Do there exist opportunities for a university to increase its knowledge of its community and its clientele? 5. To what extent will an educational activity contribute to the development of community leadership?

[17] In Lyman Bryson (ed.), *Facing the Future's Risks* (New York, 1952), 31.

[18] C. Wright Mills, *Mass Society and Liberal Education*, 181.

[19] *Encyclopedia of the Social Sciences* (New York, 1930), II, 645.

[20] Paul H. Sheats, Clarence D. Jayne, and Ralph B. Spence, *Adult Education: The Community Approach* (New York, 1953), 10

NOTES TO CHAPTER VII

[1] This is a group conclusion reached by a faculty seminar on the teaching of liberal arts for adults sponsored by the Center for the Study of Liberal Education for Adults at the University of Omaha, May 7-9, 1954.

[2] *Ibid.*

[3] A. Whitney Griswold, "Educating the Uncommon Man," in *Is the Common Man too Common?* (University of Oklahoma Press, 1954), 95, 97-98.

[4] John W. Dodds, "The Common Man on the Campus," *ibid.*, 109-110.

[5] Read Bain, "How Liberal Is the Liberal Arts College?" *American Association of University Professors Bulletin*, XXXIX (Winter, 1953-1954), 627.

[6] As quoted in the *New York Times*, January 16, 1955.

[7] Harold Taylor, *On Education and Freedom* (New York, 1954), 206-207.

[8] Lyman Bryson, *Reason and Discontent: The Task of Liberal Adult Education* (Pasadena: The Fund for Adult Education, 1954), 11.

[9] Walter R Agard in the *New York Times Magazine*, June 6, 1954, 59.

[10] *Mass Society and Liberal Education*, 19.

[11] In *Proceedings of the Association of University Evening Colleges, 1953*, 45.

[12] Interview quoted in the *New Orleans Times-Picayune*, March 26, 1954.

[13] Quoted in discussion at New Orleans conference.

[14] In *Proceedings of the Association of University Evening Colleges, 1953*, 48.

[15] *Ibid.*, 39-40. Author's italics.

[16] Courtney C. Brown, Assistant to the Chairman of the Board, Standard Oil Company of New Jersey, in *The Saturday Review*, November 21, 1953.

[17] Albert J. Nickerson, Vice-President, The Sacony-Vacuum Oil Company, in *ibid*. Author's italics.

[18] *The Saturday Review*, November 21, 1953.

[19] Brown in *ibid*.

[20] Nickerson in *ibid*.

[21] *The American Mind*, 441-443. These selections paraphrased or quoted directly.

Bibliography

Literature on the evening college is not extensive. In the preparation of this book, therefore, the author has largely relied on three types of material: (1) books and articles on the general subject of adult education and related fields, (2) publications of the Center for the Study of Liberal Education for Adults, and (3) the *Proceedings* of the Association of University Evening Colleges and of the Association of Urban Universities. Case histories have been selected from the files of evening college deans. There is included in the book also many of the author's own experiences and ideas derived from numerous workshops and discussion groups on the subject of the evening college. Perhaps he learned something, too, from several years' experience as an evening dean.

The following list is indicative of the type of material used:

ADLER, MORTIMER J. "Adult Education," *Journal of Higher Education*, XXIII, No. 2 (February 1952).

Adult Education Handbook for Administrators, University of the State of New York, Bulletin No. 1388.

Adult Education in the Modern University. A report by a special committee of N.E.A., University of Michigan Press, 1949.

Adult Leadership, published by the A.E.A. of the U.S.A.

ALLEN, FREDERICK L. *The Big Change*. New York: Harper & Brothers, 1952.

ANDERSON, C. LESTER, and GATES, ARTHUR I. "The General Nature of Learning," *49th Yearbook*, National Society for the Study of Education. Chicago: University of Chicago Press, 1950.

BALTZELL, E. DIGBY. "Bell Telephone's Experiment in Education," *Harper's*, March 1955.

BAYLEY, NANCY, and ODEN, M. H. "The Maintenance of Intellectual Ability in Gifted Adults," *Journal of Gerontology*, X, No. 1 (January 1955).

Better Teaching—Our Common Goal. University College, Washington University, St. Louis, Mo.

BITTNER, W. S. *The University Extension Movement.* Bulletin 1919, No. 84, Bureau of Education. Government Printing Office, 1920.

BRYSON, LYMAN (ed.). *Facing the Future's Risks.* New York: Harper & Brothers, 1952.

———. "The Meaning of Community Leadership." Address delivered at Community Leadership Institute, Bigwin Inn, July 1953.

BURCH, GLEN. "Evaluating Adult Education," *Adult Education Journal*, VI, No. 2 (April 1947).

CAREY, JAMES T. *Why Students Drop Out: A Study of Evening College Student Motivation.* Chicago: The Center for the Study of Liberal Education for Adults, 1953.

COLBERT, R. J. *Wisconsin's Economic Outlook*, University Extension Division, University of Wisconsin, 1953.

COMMAGER, HENRY STEELE. *The American Mind.* New Haven: Yale University Press, 1952.

DIEKHOFF, JOHN. "Time Off for Good Behavior," *Journal of General Education*, October 1952.

DODDY, HURLEY. *Informal Groups in Adult Education.* Institute of Adult Education, Teachers College, Columbia University, 1951.

ECKELBERRY, R. H. *The History of the Municipal University in the United States.* Bulletin 1932, No. 2, United States Office of Education. Washington, D.C.: Government Printing Office.

ESSERT, PAUL L. *Creative Leadership in Adult Education.* New York: Prentice-Hall, Inc., 1951.

FRANK, LAWRENCE K. *Society as the Patient.* New Brunswick: Rutgers University Press, 1948.

———. "The Concept of Maturity," *Child Development*, XXI (March 1950).

FREEMAN, FRANK S. *Individual Differences.* New York: Henry Holt & Co., 1934.

GABRIEL, RALPH H. *The Course of American Democratic Thought.* New York: Ronald Press Company, 1940.

Handbook for Teachers of Adults. Bulletin of the California State Department of Education, May 1951.

HAVIGHURST, ROBERT J. *Human Development and Education.* New York: Longmans, Green & Co., Inc., 1953.

———. *Social Roles of the Middle-Aged Person.* "Notes and Essays on Education for Adults," No. 4. Chicago: The Center for the Study of Liberal Education for Adults, 1953.

HAYAKAWA, S. I. *Adult Education as a Time-Binding Process.* "Notes and Essays on Education for Adults," No. 8. Chicago: The Center for the Study of Liberal Education for Adults, 1954.

Higher Education in the Forty Eight States. Council of State Governments, 1952.

HILGARD, ERNEST R. *Theories of Learning.* New York: Appleton-Century-Crofts, Inc., 1948.

HILGARD, ERNEST R., and RUSSELL, DAVID H. "Motivation in School Learning," *49th Yearbook*, National Society for the Study of Education. Chicago: University of Chicago Press, 1950.

HOULE, CYRIL O. "The Evening College: Its Purposes and Its Relationships Within the University." Address delivered at Annual Meeting of the Association of Urban Universities, October 1953.

———. *Introduction to Universities in Adult Education.* UNESCO, 1952.

HUNTER, FLOYD. *Community Power Structure.* Chapel Hill, N.C.: University of North Carolina Press, 1953.

HUNTER, GUY. *Developments in Residential Adult Education.* The Fund for Adult Education, 1954.

"Industry and the Liberal Arts," *The Saturday Review*, November 21, 1953.

KALLEN, HORACE. *The Liberation of the Adult*, "Notes and Essays on Education for Adults," No. 7. Chicago: The Center for the Study of Liberal Education for Adults, 1954.

KUHLEN, RAYMOND G. and others. *The Psychology of Human Development.* New York: Appleton-Century-Crofts, Inc., 1949.

LEHMAN, HARVEY C. *Age and Achievement.* Princeton: Princeton University Press, 1953.

LEWIN, KURT. "Group Decisions and Social Change," in SWANSON, GUY E., NEWCOMB, THEODORE M., and HARTLEY, EUGENE L., *Readings in Social Psychology.* New York: Henry Holt & Co., Inc., 1952.

LIVINGSTON, SIR RICHARD. "The Essentials of Education," *Atlantic Monthly*, CCIX, No. I (January 1952).

LOVE, ROBERT A. "Purposes of Evening Colleges and Relations with the Rest of the University." Address delivered at Annual Meeting, Association of Urban Universities, October 1953.

LYND, ROBERT S., *Knowledge for What?* Princeton: Princeton University Press, 1948.

LYND, ROBERT S., and MERRELL, HELEN. *Middletown in Transition: A Study in Cultural Conflicts.* New York: Harcourt, Brace & Co., 1937.

McCLUSKY, HOWARD. "The Community Approach to Adult Education," *University of Michigan School of Education Bulletin*, XV (March 1949).

McGHEE, PAUL A. *A School for Optimists*, "Notes and Essays on Education for Adults," No. 6. Chicago: The Center for the Study of Liberal Education for Adults, 1953.

———. *Higher Education and Adult Education: Four Questions*, "Notes and Essays on Education for Adults," Chicago: The Center for the Study of Liberal Education for Adults, 1953.

———. "Three Dimensions of Adult Education." Address delivered at Annual Meeting, American Council on Education, 1953.

MILLS, C. WRIGHT. *Mass Society and Liberal Education*, "Notes and Essays on Education for Adults," No. 9. Chicago: The Center for the Study of Liberal Education for Adults, 1954.

———. *White Collar: The American Middle Classes.* New York: Oxford University Press, 1951.

MORTON, JOHN R. *University Extension in the United States.* University, Ala.: University of Alabama Press, 1953.

NEUFFER, FRANK R. *Administrative Policies and Practices of Evening Colleges.* Chicago: The Center for the Study of Liberal Education for Adults, 1953.

Newsletter, Association of University Evening Colleges, 1945-1955.

Newsletter, Association of Urban Universities, 1919-1930.

OVERSTREET, HARRY. *The Mature Mind*. New York: W. W. Norton & Company, Inc., 1949.

Patterns of Liberal Education in the Evening College: A Case Study of Nine Institutions. Chicago: The Center for the Study of Liberal Education for Adults, 1952.

POWELL, JOHN WALKER, "Adult Education: American Plan," *Adult Educational Journal*, VIII, No. 3 (July 1949).

PRESSEY, SIDNEY L., JANNEY, J. ELLIOT, and KUHLEN, RAYMOND G. *Life: A Psychological Survey*. New York: Harper & Brothers, 1939.

Proceedings, Annual Meetings of Association of University Evening Colleges.

REED, BERNARD W. *Who's Who in the Association of University Evening Colleges*.

Review of Educational Research. Journal of the American Educational Research Association.

RIESMAN, DAVID. *The Lonely Crowd: A Study of the Changing American Character*. New Haven: Yale University Press, 1950.

Role of the Liberal Arts in University Evening College Curricula. Chicago: The Center for the Study of Liberal Education for Adults, 1955.

SCHWERTMAN, JOHN B. "The Need for Theory in Adult Education," *School and Society*, June 27, 1953.

SHEATS, PAUL H., JAYNE, CLARENCE D., and SPENCE, RALPH B. *Adult Education: The Community Approach*. New York: The Dryden Press, Inc., 1953.

SIEGLE, PETER E. "Mountains, Plateaus, and Valleys in Adult Learning," *Adult Education, IV*, No. 4 (March 1954).

SNOW, ROBERT H. *Community Adult Education*. New York: G. P. Putnam's Sons, 1955.

STERN, BERNARD H. *How Much Does Adult Experience Count?* Chicago: The Center for the Study of Liberal Education for Adults, 1955.

STRONG, EDWARD K. *Change of Interest with Age*. Stanford, Calif.: Stanford University Press, 1931.

THORNDIKE, EDWARD L. *Adult Interests*. New York: The Macmillan Co., 1935.

THORNDIKE, EDWARD L., BREGMAN, ELSIE O., TILTON, J. WARREN, and WOODYARD, ELLA. *Adult Learning.* New York: The Macmillan Co., 1928.

TYLER, RALPH W. *Basic Principles of Curriculum and Instruction.* Chicago: University of Chicago Press, 1950.

WARNER, W. LLOYD, and ASSOCIATES. *Democracy in Jonesville.* New York: Harper & Brothers, 1949.

WRONG, DENNIS H. "The Stork Surprises the Demographers," *Commentary,* October 1952.

Index

Absenteeism, 11

ACE Psychological Test, 18-19

Adams, Herbert Baxter, 34

Admission requirements, *see* Evening college

Adult learning, 12-19; nature of, 16-17

Agard, Walter R., 177

Akron, University of, *see* University of Akron

American College Entrance Test, *see* ACE Psychological Test

American Legion, 144, 145

Association of University Evening Colleges, 7, 30, 39-40, 46, 50, 51, 114

Association of Urban Universities, 38

Bain, Read, 170

Beard, Charles A., 152

Beard, Mary E., 152

Blackwell, Gordon, 59, 61-64, 66, 78

Brooklyn College, 35, 94, 95, 97, 100

Bryce, Lord James, 36

Bryson, Lyman, 176

Buffalo, University of, *see* University of Buffalo

Cambridge University, 35, 88

Center for the Study of Liberal Education for Adults, 18, 46, 47

Chautauqua, 33, 35, 76

Chesterton, G. K., 156

Chicago, University of, *see* University of Chicago

Cincinnati, University of, *see* University of Cincinnati

City College of New York, 35

Cleveland College, Western Reserve University, 30

College of Charleston, 35

Commager, Henry Steele, 183

Community, needs of, 58-66

Cooper Union, 36

Cosmopolitan, 36

Courses, *see* Evening college

Credit load, *see* Evening college

Curriculum, 81-111; construction, 90-92; revision, 102-111

Curti, Merle, 32

Dallas College, Southern Methodist University, 30

202

Dean, 112-137; and curriculum, 83; line of responsibility, 41

Degree program, *see* Evening college

Detroit, University of, *see* University of Detroit

Division of General Education, New York University, 28

Dodds, John W., 170

Drufner, Vincent H., 39

Education, liberal, *see* Liberal education

Educational Service Sophomore Comprehensive General Culture Test, 19

Eliot, Charles W., 36

Evening college: admission requirements, 43; and the community, 53-80; budget, 42; courses offered, 42; credit load, 44; degree program, 42; development of, 27-52; enrollment, 41; functional classification of, 27-29; future role for, 138-167; nomenclature, 30; teaching methods, 120-122; tuition, 43. *See also* Community, Curriculum, Dean, Faculty, Scholastic achievement, Student

Everybody's, 36

Faculty, 112-137; attitudes toward evening college, 122-125; how recruited, 44

Folger Shakespeare Library, 156

Frank, Lawrence K., 105

Freeman, Frank S., 13

Forums, 36

Fund for Adult Education, 46

General Federation of Women's Clubs, 36

Griswold, A. Whitney, 169, 170

Harper, William Rainey, 34

Harvard Classics, 36

Havighurst, Robert J., 62-64, 66, 105

Hesburgh, Rev. Theodore M., 171

Houle, Cyril O., 41, 50, 105

Hughes, Everett, 178

Hunter College, 35

Iowa State College, 13

Janney, J. Elliot, 13

Johns Hopkins University, 30, 34, 37

Kallen, Horace, 178, 180

Kuhlen, Raymond G., 13-16

League of Women Voters, 68

Liberal education, 162-183

Livingstone, Sir Richard, 164

Louisville, University of, *see* University of Louisville

McClure's, 36

McCoy College, Johns Hopkins University, 30, 37

McGhee, Paul, 164

Malinowski, B. K., 162

Miami University (Florida), 170

Millard Fillmore College, University of Buffalo, 30

Mills, C. Wright, 149, 161, 178

Municipal University of Omaha, 35

National Association of Manufacturers, 154

New York, City College of, *see* City College of New York

New York University, 28

North Carolina, University of, *see* University of North Carolina

Notre Dame, University of, *see* University of Notre Dame

Oxford University, 33, 85

Parent-Teachers Association, *see* PTA

Pearson's, 36

Pound, Dean Roscoe, 178

Pressey, Sidney L., 13

PTA, 60, 148

Roosevelt University, 18, 19

Sarah Lawrence College, 175

Scholastic achievement, 12-19

School of General Studies, Brooklyn College, 94

Siegle, Peter E., 16

Smith, Adam, 86

Southern Methodist University, 30

Stanford University, 170

Steffens, Lincoln, 36

Strong, E. K., Jr., 105

Student, 3-26; age range, 7; attendance, 11; day and evening compared, 11-19; median age of, 7; motivation of, 8-11; scholastic achievement, 12-19; social backgrounds of, 8, 142-144

Syracuse University, 13

Tarbell, Ida M., 36

Taylor, Frederick W., 148

Taylor, Harold, 175

Teaching methods, 120-122

Television, as medium of adult education, 76-78

Toledo, University of, *see* University of Toledo

Tyler, Ralph W., 90

United States Chamber of Commerce, 154

Universities, municipal, 35

University College, University of Chicago, 28, 37

University of Akron, 35

University of Buffalo, 30

University of Chicago, 28, 34, 37, 62

University of Cincinnati, 35, 39

University of Detroit, 35

University of Louisville, 35

University of North Carolina, 59

University of Notre Dame, 171

University of Toledo, 35

University of Wisconsin, 37, 38, 108

Warner, W. Lloyd, 142

Wertenberger, Rev. Henry J., 178

Western Reserve University, 30

Wichita Municipal University, 35

Wisconsin, University of, *see* University of Wisconsin

Wright, Louis Booker, 156

Yale University, 169

YMCA, 33, 36

Most adult education programs are supplementary to day college programs because of the wide range of its students program with vocational experience, motivation, needs and cultural aspirations it cannot derive it could be from day college programs.

b